PCs made easy

STAGE 3

A PRACTICAL COURSE

PCs made easy

STAGE 3

A PRACTICAL COURSE

PUBLISHED BY THE READER'S DIGEST ASSOCIATION LIMITED
LONDON   NEW YORK   SYDNEY   MONTREAL

PCS MADE EASY
A PRACTICAL COURSE – STAGE 3

Published by the Reader's Digest Association Limited, 2000

Reprinted with amendments, 2001

The Reader's Digest Association Limited
11 Westferry Circus, Canary Wharf, London E14 4HE
www.readersdigest.co.uk

We are committed to both the quality of our products and the service we
provide to our customers, so please feel free to contact us on 08705 113366,
or by email at cust_service@readersdigest.co.uk
If you have any comments about the content of our books, you can
contact us at gbeditorial@readersdigest.co.uk

For Reader's Digest
Series Editor: Christine Noble
Art Editor: Julie Bennett
Assistant Editor: Caroline Boucher

Reader's Digest General Books
Editorial Director: Cortina Butler
Art Director: Nick Clark

PCs made easy was created and produced for
The Reader's Digest Association Limited by De Agostini UK Ltd,
from material originally published as the Partwork
Computer Success Plus.

Printing and binding: Printer Industria Gráfica S.A., Barcelona

ISBN 0 276 42501 4

CONTENTS

Windows

Keep a healthy hard disk

With Windows' disk tools, you can ensure your computer is always achieving its optimum performance by preventing problems and putting them right if they occur.

A computer is a complicated, fragile piece of equipment, and every now and then things can and do go wrong. It can get accidentally knocked, for example, just like other electrical equipment in your home. When a PC is switched on, even what might seem like a small knock could affect the computer's hard disk, where all your programs and documents are stored. Such knocks can interfere with the data that is stored on the disk and this could make a single file – or even whole areas of the hard disk – impossible to use. As a result, any data stored there could be lost.

● Don't just switch off

Similar problems often arise when the PC is switched off before open documents are closed. Make sure that everyone using your computer – especially any children who share it – knows that the only safe way to switch a computer off is to select the Shut Down option from the Start menu. If you do this, Windows will check to ensure that any open documents have been properly saved before shutting down.

Less frequently, hard disk problems can also occur as a result of faulty software, quite outside your control.

Even when it is working properly, your computer's hard disk can become clogged up. As a result of this, you might find that it seems to slow down, and operating open and save commands takes longer than it did when the PC was new.

All these problems are easily cured with Windows' suite of programs called System Tools. There's a tool to deal with each problem.

● Instant cures

When a document file stored on disk has been damaged, it is said to be corrupted. Sometimes the file won't be accessible at all: you might,

for example, see an error message appear when you try to open a corrupted letter in Word. Even if the document isn't that important, you should always repair the damage to the disk so that it cannot affect other documents in the future. The ScanDisk tool can check your hard disk for errors and will automatically repair any it finds.

If your computer seems to be running slower than it used to, you can tune it up and get it back up to speed by using the Disk Defragmenter. This reorganizes the data on your hard disk so that programs can start, and your documents can be opened or saved, as quickly as possible. It doesn't change the way you have arranged the documents and folders on your disk, so you'll still find everything where you left it.

We'll also look at Disk Cleanup, another of Windows' System Tools. This program can automatically delete unused and unwanted files that are taking up disk space.

PC TIPS

Backing up

It's a fact of life that computers can, unfortunately, go wrong and your data – Word letters, Excel workbooks or graphic layouts, for example – might be lost. Because of this, you should always keep copies of your important documents on floppy or, if more storage memory is needed, on Zip disks.

Checking your hard disk for errors

If you suspect that files on your hard disk have become damaged or corrupted, a simple-to-use Windows program called ScanDisk might solve the problem.

ANY OF the files and data stored on your hard drive can become corrupted. In most cases you can repair this damage, although it is likely that the files can only be recycled as free space rather than reclaimed. ScanDisk is the tool to use for such tasks.

1 To start ScanDisk, press the Start button and select Accessories from the Programs menu. Select System Tools from the Accessories menu and single click on the ScanDisk icon.

2 The ScanDisk dialog box lets you select which drive to check. Select the C: drive by clicking on the relevant item in the list of drives.

PC TIPS

What causes disk errors?

Most disk errors are caused by human error. For example, moving the computer while it is switched on can cause problems. Always make sure you go through the correct shut-down process before you switch off your computer.

However, if your computer freezes up completely, you might not be able to shut down correctly, so your only option might be to switch your PC off. If you have to do this, your computer should notice that it wasn't shut down correctly and will automatically check your hard disk the next time you restart it. This adds only a few minutes to the start-up time.

3 You have the choice of a Standard or Thorough disk scan. The Standard option checks only the files and folders stored on the hard disk, whereas the Thorough option also checks the physical surface of the hard disk. Most of the time you should choose a Standard scan, the quickest of the two options. You will only need to select a Thorough scan if you want to make absolutely sure there are no errors, or if you have already detected errors through a Standard scan.

4 After selecting a Standard scan, make sure that the final tick box, labelled Automatically fix errors, is checked. Press the Start button. ScanDisk works through the disk without asking you to confirm any disk repairs it needs to do.

5 ScanDisk will now begin to scan the hard disk. You will see several stages indicated by the progress bar that appears at the bottom of the dialog box.

6 When ScanDisk has finished checking your hard disk, you will see a panel of information. Most of this is only of interest to computer experts, but the first line will tell you about any errors ScanDisk found.

If ScanDisk finds damaged areas of the disk, it will try to read the information stored there and save it to a safe place on your hard disk. These 'rescued' files are usable only by computer experts, however, so you will have to rely on back-up copies of affected documents.

Note: if you selected a Thorough scan, the ScanDisk process will take a much longer time to complete – anything from 30 minutes to a few hours, depending on the size of your computer's hard disk and the amount of material stored on it.

CHECKPOINT ✔

GIVE YOUR COMPUTER A MEDICAL

☑ If you're running Windows 98, you can use its Maintenance Wizard to keep your PC in good working condition. You can also schedule regular check-ups using the ScanDisk and Disk Defragmenter System Tools.
☑ If you're using Windows 95, you need to schedule and perform these checks yourself. Use ScanDisk (see the example on this page) whenever you suspect there is a hard disk problem with your computer. ScanDisk runs quickly and the Standard scan will alert you to any major problems that might exist. You need only do a longer Thorough scan every six months or so. Most people need only run the standard Disk Defragmenter every four months. But if you install lots of programs or games, consider doing it every two months.

Defragmenting your hard disk

Your hard disk can slow down as more programs and files are stored on it, but a simple operation will soon have it running as quickly as possible.

YOUR HARD disk can slow down as it tries to keep up with all the files stored on it. This problem – fragmentation – is not too serious but can be avoided if you use Windows' Disk Defragmenter tool to reorganize your hard disk. It does this by moving files around on the hard disk. Don't worry about not being able to find them: the files appear in exactly the same place, but your hard disk can now find them more quickly.

1 To start Disk Defragmenter, press the Start button and select Accessories from the Programs menu. Select System Tools from the Accessories menu and click on the third option of the drop-down menu: Disk Defragmenter.

2 You will be asked to select the drive you want to defragment. First, though, click the settings button.

3 In the dialog box that appears, make sure that the First option is ticked. This lets Windows optimize the performance of your PC. Click the OK button and then click OK again to proceed.

4 The defragmentation process will start and you can see it happening by watching the progress bar in the centre of the dialog box. You can run other programs at the same time, but you'll find your system will operate rather more slowly while defragmentation is going on. To see how the hard disk is being rearranged, click the Show Details button.

5 Now you can get a visual idea of what the Disk Defragmenter tool is doing. The small squares represent one cluster of data on the hard disk. Press the Legend button (inset) and you'll see a pop-up panel that describes what each of the different colours refers to.

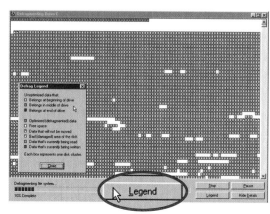

6 When the process is finished (the larger your hard disk and the more information that's stored on it, the longer it will take), a dialog box will appear, asking if you now want to quit Disk Defragmenter. Press the OK button. You should now notice a marked improvement in the performance of your computer.

WHAT IT MEANS

FRAGMENTATION

All computer disks are divided into many thousands of sections, known as clusters. Windows uses these clusters to store clumps of information from files. The most efficient way to store this information is when the clusters are next to each other on the disk. The disk can then read and write them faster. However, as you save and delete files and install and delete programs, files will be split into several fragments and widely scattered over the disk. Some fragmentation is normal, and fragmented files still work perfectly well – they just take longer to open and save. However, if fragmentation affects a lot of files and programs on your hard disk, the decrease in your PC's speed can be marked. Defragmenting the disk puts the files into a more organized physical order.

Cleaning up your hard disk

As you use your computer, many files are created that you will never need again. Here we see how to get rid of them to free up valuable disk space.

WINDOWS COMES with Disk Cleanup, a special program that automatically roots out useless old files in just a few minutes, saving you many megabytes of hard disk space in the process. When you run Disk Cleanup, it lets you choose which types of file to look for and delete. You can, for example, select temporary files created when you access the Internet.

1 To run Disk Cleanup, click on the Start button and select Accessories from the Programs menu. Select System Tools from the Accessories menu and click on Disk Cleanup.

2 In the Select Drive dialog box that appears, make sure that drive C: (if this is your hard drive) is selected, not the floppy disk. Then press the OK button.

3 Disk Cleanup shows you the types of files it can clean up. Initially, only two options are ticked. Temporary Internet Files and Downloaded Program Files cover the different types of files – Web pages, graphics and so on – that are stored on your PC from your travels on the Internet. It's easy to collect several thousand in just a week's browsing.

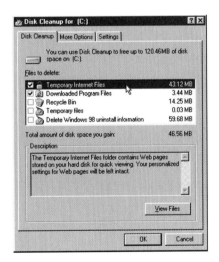

4 Tick the Temporary files option if you want to delete the various files that programs such as Word create behind the scenes. Well-behaved programs delete such files automatically, but crashes can cause the programs to forget this task.

5 If you upgraded from Windows 95 to Windows 98, the setup program probably stored your old Windows 95 setup – just in case Windows 98 didn't work properly and you needed to uninstall it. Once your PC has been running Windows 98 without problems, it's safe to delete the old files. Tick the Delete Windows 98 uninstall information option to do this.

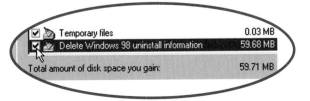

6 Press the OK button and confirm your choice when Windows asks you to. It then deletes the various files you have identified as being redundant. It takes only a few minutes to recover the disk space.

Installing new software

Whenever you buy a new piece of software, you have to load it from the CD-ROM or floppy disk onto your PC's hard disk. Here we show you how easy it is to install new programs.

Loading or 'installing' new software is much the same as putting any new data onto your PC from a CD-ROM or floppy disk. But instead of copying the files yourself, your PC will run a set-up program to install the new program on your PC's hard disk for you.

When you insert the new program disk and go through the installation process, all you are doing is transferring these instructions, bit by bit from the floppy or CD-ROM disk, onto your PC's hard disk. Once they are on the PC, they provide it with a new range of instructions that you can use directly, just as you use any of the programs already installed on your PC when you bought it.

● Hard disk space

With a small piece of software, you might be transferring only a few files. With a major software package, you might be transferring most of a CD-ROM's contents. It depends on how the program will be used. Reference programs that provide you with data, images and sounds, such as Microsoft's Encarta, require only a little hard disk space because the program reads the data directly from the CD-ROM disk (the CD-ROM actually needs to be in the CD-ROM drive for the program to access the information on it). But major programs, such as Word or CorelDRAW, can take up over 100MB of space on your hard disk when they are fully installed on your PC.

● Installation time

The time it takes to load software varies from program to program. Clearly the larger the program, the longer it takes to load. But some major programs take much longer to install

than others as they ask a lot of questions before they even begin to install the files. This is because these types of programs are also used in offices where it is important to know who is using the software and whether it has been properly licensed. Even with the largest programs, though, the installation process rarely takes more than half an hour – and is usually much quicker.

Successful Installation

World Reference Atlas has been successfully installed on your computer.

To run World Reference Atlas, simply double click on its icon in the DK Multimedia group in Program Manager.

Be sure to send in the registration information for your new software.

OK

You'll be able to install most software successfully simply by inserting the CD-ROM supplied and following the instructions given by Windows.

● Installation options

Most programs let you choose how much of the software you wish to install, but most home users usually install the entire program. With the CorelDRAW program, for example, the default option for installation is called Typical and, as the name suggests, it will install all the files that most people typically use. Other options are Compact, which installs only the essential

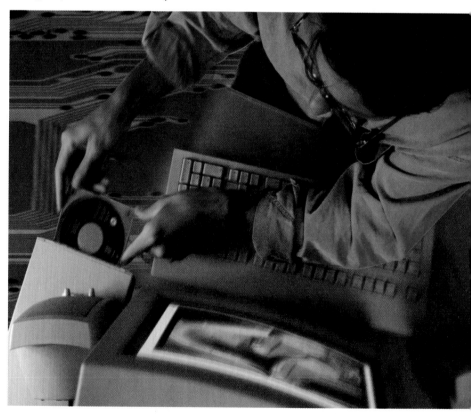

Installing a new program can often seem daunting, but usually it involves nothing more than answering a few on-screen questions put to you by Windows. Any changes to your PC set-up are made automatically.

Installing new software will seem less of a daunting prospect when you understand what happens during the installation process.

Checking available space

Before you install a new program, you must ensure that there is enough space for it on your hard disk. The box in which the software comes will tell you how much space it will take up. You can check how much is available for it on your hard disk by double-clicking on the My Computer icon, then clicking on the C: icon with the right mouse button. Select Properties from the list of Options that appears and you'll see your hard disk displayed as a pie chart (left), showing the way your hard disk space is being used. The lighter area shows how much space is free, while the darker area shows the amount of space currently taken up with other files.

files to save disk space, and Custom, which allows you to choose exactly which files to install. The Custom option is really intended for advanced users. Unless you have very little space on your hard disk, it's best to use the Typical option. This also applies when installing other Windows programs.

● Installing other software

Most large programs have a number of extra applications as well as the main program functions. These include items such as fonts and clip-art. While you should install all the main program functions, check how much space these extra files take up before you install them. If they take up a lot of memory, they might not leave you with much room to install anything else on your hard disk. If you think they are simply going to clog up your hard disk, you can leave all these items on the CD-ROM. If you are in any doubt, *always* leave them on the CD-ROM – you can install them when and if you need them at a later date.

All you have to do to start most of the software you are likely to buy is to insert the CD-ROM. This starts the

The icon for the CD-ROM drive features an image of a CD-ROM, with the letter that signifies the drive underneath it.

program responsible for managing the installation process. If you have any older software programs that you also want to install, they might not include the special autostart software that is a necessary requirement. If this is the case, there is no other option but to install the software manually, which is a more time-consuming process. The same techniques are also used to install programs from floppy disks.

HARDWARE REQUIREMENTS

Whenever you buy new software, make sure you check its hardware requirements first to ensure your PC is able to run it. Here's a summary of CoralDRAW's requirements:
- ☑ Windows 95, 98 or NT
- ☑ 133MHz Pentium processor
- ☑ 32MB RAM (64 recommended)
- ☑ At least 100MB of hard disk space for the basic CoralDRAW program.
- ☑ CD-ROM drive
- ☑ Super VGA display

WHY RESTART YOUR PC?

Some programs will ask you to restart your computer once a program has been installed. This is because they have installed special files that work closely with Windows. For technical reasons, Windows needs to close down and restart before they can work. Only then will you be able to run your new software properly.

How to Install CorelDRAW from CD-ROM

In Stage 2, pages 68–89, we introduced you to the graphics program CorelDRAW. Here we show you how to install the program from CD-ROM, a process that involves steps common to other installation programs.

1 To start the installation, you need to insert the CorelDRAW CD-ROM labelled 1 into your CD-ROM drive. The CD-ROM will autostart and a window will appear, giving you several options. Click the Install option.

2 The Install program will then analyse your system (to see how much memory you have, how fast your processor is and so on). When it's finished, another window will appear, asking if you are sure you want to continue. To do so, press the Next button.

3 The next window displays the License Agreement, which asks you to agree not to copy or lend the software illegally. The following window asks you to type in your name and the name of your company (if relevant). This information is not really essential and merely helps to register the product. Press the Next button and a window will give you a chance to check your entry; press Next if everything is correct.

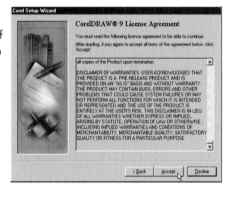

4 The next screen asks you to enter the product serial code for your copy of CorelDRAW; this code is different for each copy of the software and it is important that you don't lose it (the code is printed on a registration card that you'll find in the CorelDRAW box). It is a good idea to copy it down somewhere else in case you lose the original. When you've typed in the code, press the Next button to go on.

5 You will now be presented with the installation options. There are three options from which to choose. The Typical installation will be selected for you by CorelDRAW by default, so press Next to proceed.

6 The installation program checks to see what spelling dictionary you want to use. Make sure the right one is selected before proceeding.

7 A new window asks you exactly where you want to install the software. CorelDRAW suggests the best location, so simply click Next to move to the next step. Click the Yes button when asked to confirm this step.

8 Click the Next button when the program asks you which Start menu Folder to use for the CorelDRAW programs. Then click the Install button on the next screen.

9 The following windows are the final parts of the set-up process. There is a progress window showing how the transfer of instructions is going (right above). When this is finished, you will be asked by the program if you want to register the software online, but you can do this at a later date. When a window tells you that your installation is complete, click OK. The final step is to restart Windows (see Why Restart Your PC? box, opposite).

Installing software manually

Sometimes your PC won't automatically know you are trying to install a new program. All this means is that you have to make a few extra choices and inputs yourself.

SOME SOFTWARE doesn't start automatically – this means you will have to find the set-up or install file on the CD-ROM (the software manual will tell you the exact name of the file to look for). Here we show you how easy it is to load new programs on to your PC manually.

1 For software that doesn't autostart, you need to locate the set-up or install file on the CD-ROM. To do this, go to the My Computer icon on your Desktop (right) and double-click on it.

2 When the My Computer window opens, you will be able to see the CD-ROM drive. It has a small picture of a CD-ROM and the letter that the drive has been designated is underneath (in this case, D:). Double-click on the icon to open the CD-ROM drive window.

3 The contents of the CD-ROM will then be displayed. Often, the file you need to double-click on to start the set-up process will be called Setup and you'll spot it straight away. Sometimes, this file is called Install and you might have to look through many files and folders to find it.

4 When you double-click on the Setup (or Install) file, the installation process begins. As the installation proceeds, you might have to answer some simple questions about your computer's set-up, or confirm that the software is making acceptable choices about where and how it will work on your computer.

PC TIPS

Finding the right file

Sometimes when you click on the (D:) icon to view the contents of a CD-ROM, you can find yourself presented with a whole page of files (right). You can organize these to make it easier to find the file you need by going to the View menu, selecting Arrange Icons and then clicking on by Name (right). All the files on the CD-ROM will then appear in alphabetical order, making it easier for you to find the Setup file.

Another method to start manual installation

1 If a program you have just bought doesn't install automatically and you don't like the manual method shown above, here's another way to do it. Click on the Start button and choose Run from the menu that appears.

2 Now Windows needs to know the location of the file, so click on the Browse button.

3 Then you will see a dialog box that allows you to look at the contents of your hard disk and the other disk drives on your computer. Choose your CD-ROM drive from the pull-down menu at the top of the screen.

4 It is now just a matter of locating the file that starts the set-up process. Remember that in most cases this involves running a computer program that monitors the installation process for you, so it will be called either Install.exe or Setup.exe. Double-click on this file to begin the installation process.

Installing new typefaces

You don't have to stick to the typefaces that come with Windows. By adding new typefaces to your computer – either those that come with new programs or others that you buy separately – you can give your work a new look.

Among the first fun things you can try with a word processor are the different typefaces (called fonts) installed on your computer. Experimenting with curious-sounding Arial, Algerian or the more traditional Times New Roman is great fun.

Windows comes with several fonts, but when you install some new programs you might have the option of adding more. Some printers even include new fonts. However, sometimes you might find that you need to use a particular font that isn't on your system. For example, you might need a solid, chunky font for headlines in your club newsletter, or an elegant, script-like typeface to create imposing-looking prize certificates for the school sports day.

Windows comes with a number of typefaces that you can use in almost any program. You can also add your own.

You will find that changing fonts can radically alter the look and tone of your text. Some fonts are simple and clear, others more ornate, or more eye-catching, as used in posters. You should also beware of using too many strikingly different fonts in any one document. More than two or three typefaces in a letter or document is likely to make it look a mess.

● Adding new typefaces

Some software adds new fonts for you, but you can also install them using the Windows Control Panel. The fonts will be copied from the CD-ROM or floppy disk to your hard disk. Once you've added your new fonts, you'll find that they are available in almost all your Windows programs – not just the programs they came with.

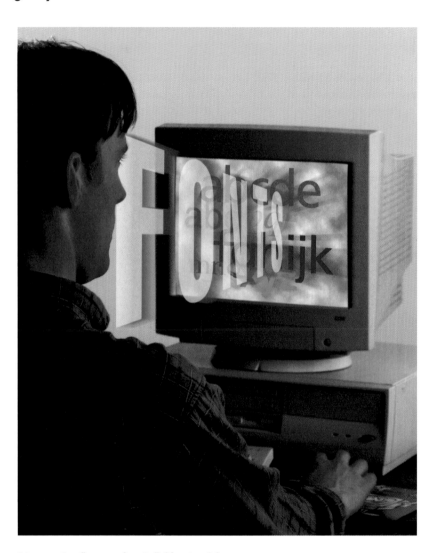

It's easy to install new typefaces (called fonts), and there are even some on your original Windows CD-ROM that you can install right now.

WHY ARE THERE SO MANY TYPEFACES?

Some typefaces have many subtle variations. Arial, for instance, is made up of several slightly different typefaces, all created from the same basic shape: Arial, Arial bold, Arial italic and Arial bold italic. If you create a letter using the Arial typeface and then use Word's bold button, Word uses the Arial bold variation to form the letters on your screen and on the printed page. These closely related variations make up a font 'family'. Programs such as Word 'hide' these simple variations from you: you need only choose the basic typeface and then decide whether you want bold, italic or both.

Adding new fonts

New fonts are supplied on program disks or as special font disks. To see what's involved in installing them, we'll add two fonts from the Windows CD-ROM.

1 Open up the Control Panel and double-click on the Fonts icon. This icon doesn't start a program; instead it's a shortcut to a special Fonts folder on your hard disk.

2 The Fonts folder appears and you'll see the fonts installed on your computer. They might be displayed in list form or as small icons. This is how the folder appears in large icon form (an option in the View menu).

3 To install a new font, click on the File menu and then select the Install New Font command from the drop-down list of options.

4 You'll see the Add Fonts dialog box. Initially, the listed Fonts box says 'No fonts found'. This is because it always starts by looking on your C: drive. We'll add some fonts from the Windows CD-ROM. Insert it into your CD-ROM drive and then select your CD-ROM drive from the Drives list (right).

5 Use the Folders list and double-click on the tools folder, then click on reskit, the desktop and the minitel folder. Windows will find two fonts and list them at the top of the dialog box. Note: there are several slightly different versions of the Windows CD-ROM; it is possible that yours will not have these files or it might have different files.

6 Pick the fonts you want to add. To select a single font, you need only click on it to highlight it. However, in this exercise we want to add both fonts. The simplest way to do this is to press the Select All button and then press the OK button. As soon as you do so, Windows will copy the fonts into your Fonts folder.

7 To use one of your new fonts, start Word. From the Font list, choose Arial Alternative (or the name of any of the fonts you have found and added). Now, whatever text you type will be in the new font.

SYMBOL TYPEFACES

The Arial Alternative Symbol font added above is used for special symbols (shown below) rather than text. You can select it from the Font list (Step 7) or you can use it via the Symbol command from Word's Insert menu.

Installing Windows' extra programs

Windows is not just one program: it's made up of many different programs. Most will have been copied to your computer's hard disk when it was built, but some very useful programs are contained on the Windows CD-ROM for you to add if you need them.

If you have used several computers, you might find that Windows varies slightly from one to the next. Although the basic operations are the same, you will probably have noticed that some of the minor functions are different. For example, it is possible that the Backup program (which allows you to copy your work files from the computer to a series of floppy disks) is present on one PC, but missing from another.

This happens for two reasons. First, PC manufacturers might choose slightly different installation options when copying the Windows files to the computer's hard disk. Subtle differences also show up because Microsoft has released several updated versions of Windows since Windows 95 was launched in August 1995.

● Typical installations
Most of the time, PC makers add Windows to the computer through a 'typical' installation. This copies only the most commonly used programs to the computer's hard disk, ready for you to use. There are many other components, however, which are not copied in the typical installation. Most of the time, you won't even notice they are missing, but it is useful to know how components help Windows work, what types of extra components are available on your Windows CD-ROM and how to load them on to your computer when you need them.

● Loading extra components
A component is a specific part of Windows that can be added or removed from your computer without affecting how the rest of Windows works. The most important components are installed as standard, but some of the less essential ones are not.

These uninstalled components are not necessarily any less useful than the others, but might be specific to a particular type of computer. For example, you do not need the components that control sound if you don't have a Multimedia computer. Some components are left uninstalled because they are of interest only to more experienced computer users. For example, business users with networks can load components that check how their computers are being shared between different users.

Several uninstalled components are left out merely because they are a little frivolous – and leaving them out saves hard disk space. For example, Windows has some sounds and pictures that are fun to add but are not really essential for the efficient operating of the computer, unless you have disk space to spare.

● Important components
However, there are also times when adding certain components can be very useful. For example, it is well worth having the Character

Map program to help you to add special characters and symbols to your documents.

Although the Character Map component comes on the Windows CD-ROM, it's not normally installed at the same time as Windows. Here, we'll show how to add this mini-program to your computer as an example of how to add any extra component.

You need to install the extra Windows components by using a different method from the way you install other new software (see pages 12–15). Instead, you use a special part of the Add/Remove Programs tool that is located in the Control Panel. The Add/Remove Programs tool keeps track of all the Windows components that have already been installed on your computer. It can also quickly show you what other options are available on the Windows CD-ROM.

The Add/Remove Programs tool

It is worth learning how to use this important tool properly, as it can be used for a variety of housekeeping tasks that will help to keep Windows running smoothly.

To start the Add/Remove Programs tool, first open the Control Panel (above) and then double-click on the Add/Remove Programs icon (below).

THE ADD/REMOVE Programs tool handles many Windows housekeeping tasks. With it you can install or uninstall programs and add or remove Windows components. You can also use it to create a special floppy disk, which can help if your computer has problems starting Windows, or to solve emergencies.

You start the tool through the Control Panel (left). You will then see a dialog box with three tabs at the top: Install/Uninstall; Windows Setup and Startup Disk (right).

With the first tab, you can remove unwanted programs from your computer's hard disk. You might want to do this to recover some hard disk space from programs you no longer need or to remove a program that isn't working correctly (see page 11). You should always use this option to remove programs, instead of just deleting them by dragging them into the Recycle Bin.

On the page opposite we've shown how to use the second tab – Windows Setup – to add components from the Windows CD-ROM.

The third tab has just one button, Create Disk. You use this to make a special floppy disk called a Startup Disk. This stores important system files that Windows can use to restart the PC properly if a problem occurs with your hard disk.

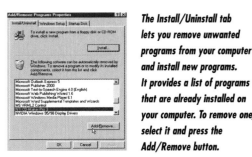

The Install/Uninstall tab lets you remove unwanted programs from your computer and install new programs. It provides a list of programs that are already installed on your computer. To remove one, select it and press the Add/Remove button.

The Windows Setup tab provides a way to load the many components that are supplied with the Windows CD-ROM.

You need only use the last option once: it will create a special floppy disk for use in emergencies. Keep this Startup Disk somewhere safe. Should Windows not start up correctly, you can use this disk to get going again.

Installing the Character Map program

The Character Map program is one of the more useful extra components in Windows. It is easy to install and takes up only a small amount of hard disk space.

THE CHARACTER MAP program is a useful tool that you can use to see the full range of letters, numbers and symbols in your fonts. Once installed, you can call it up to view the contents of any font on your PC. You can copy and paste characters from Character Map into your documents – even if the program doesn't have an Insert Symbol command.

1 Open the Add/ Remove Programs dialog box, as shown opposite, and click on the Windows Setup tab. This displays a list of Components. Items that have a tick are already installed on your computer; those without have not yet been installed.

2 We want to install the Character Map tool, which Windows classifies as a System Tool. Click on this item and then press the Details button (inset) to see further information on this option.

3 The System Tools window appears and lists all the individual components available. In this case, there are several tools, some of which are already installed.

4 Click on the box next to Character Map to add a tick. Press the OK button to return to the previous dialog box.

5 Windows returns you to the Add/Remove Programs dialog box. Click the OK button.

6 After a moment, you will be asked to insert the Windows CD-ROM into your computer's CD-ROM drive. Press the OK button and you will see a progress window to confirm the copying process.

7 Once the copying has finished, the Add/Remove Programs tool will close automatically. Use the Start button to look in the Accessories folder. Click on the System Tools and you will see that the Character Map component has been added to the menu of programs.

Windows' extra components

Windows comes with a number of extra components which are not part of a typical installation. Here is a selection of some that might prove useful.

ALL OF THESE fun and functional options are included on your original Windows CD-ROM. These programs can be installed on your hard disk by following the procedure used to install the Character Map.

● Multimedia Sound Schemes
We have already shown how an external microphone can be attached to your computer for recording new sounds (see Stage 1, page 89). However, if you don't have a microphone, or don't want to be bothered recording new sounds, then you can use the collections of alternative sound effects offered by Windows.

Each collection of sounds follows certain themes, such as wild animals, robots and so on. If you install and select them, they will replace the sounds that you hear.

● Direct cable connection
This useful program lets you connect two PCs together using a cable. You can then transfer files from one to the other. It's a lot faster than swapping floppy disks between two PCs and you can transfer any size of file (floppies can accommodate files up to 1.4Mb in size only).

● Quick View
Quick View is a useful program that enables you to preview a document without having to open it in the program that created it. The advantage of this is that Quick View is very fast, so it's easy to use if you are searching for a particular file where you know the contents but not the name. Quick View works not only with many types of text files but also with picture files, such as those created by the Microsoft Paint program.

Quick View can show you the contents of files much more quickly than the program that created them can open them for editing.

If you can't find Windows' built-in games, check in the Games section of the Accessories components.

● Games
Windows is supplied with a number of games. These are entertaining enough, but comprise simple card games and beat-the-clock routines, rather than action games.

● Clipboard Viewer
Some of these smaller programs are left out of the typical installation because they 'clog up' the Start menu and can be confusing to first-time users. The Clipboard Viewer is one of the items left out. It's a tiny program that allows you to view any information that you have copied to the Clipboard. This can occasionally be useful if you need to check what is in the Clipboard before pasting it into a new position.

DIFFERENT VERSIONS OF WINDOWS

There are several different installation modes for Windows. Each one takes up varying amounts of disk space and installs a different number of components. Depending on the one used when your PC was built, you might find differences in which components have been installed. For example, on most PCs, Windows 95 takes up little more than 50MB of hard disk space, no matter which options you choose. Windows 98, by contrast, requires lots more space. For example, if you upgraded from Windows 95 to Windows 98, you typically need 260MB. The exact figure depends on your PC's configuration and the options chosen when Windows was installed. When Windows 98 is supplied already installed on a new PC, however, the amount of hard disk space is rather lower – typically 210MB. On some PCs, the amount required can be as much as 400MB, depending on the hard disk type and the number of options and components chosen.

Windows timekeeping

Your computer's clock keeps going even when you switch off your PC. It knows when you load programs and when you save files. Here's your guide to how Windows keeps track of time and, therefore, your work.

Once the correct time has been entered into your computer, all the changes you make to your documents will be timestamped by the PC's internal clock.

Keeping track of the time and date, even when the computer is switched off, is an important function that your computer performs almost invisibly. The small clock in the bottom right corner of the Windows screen might be the only thing you have noticed that indicates your computer's timekeeping.

The ability to tell the time comes from your computer's internal clock. This clock has its own battery that keeps the clock ticking, even if you don't use your PC for several months. The time stored in this clock is displayed on the toolbar in Windows to give you a convenient on-screen clock to refer to while you're working.

● Clocking on

Windows also uses the clock for its own purposes to timestamp and datestamp files and folders every time you create, modify or save them. You can see how this works at its simplest by double-clicking on the My Computer icon to open the My Computer window. From this window, open your computer's hard disk (C: drive) folder by double-clicking on it. Inside, you'll see a number of folders. Move your mouse pointer to the

If you go to the View menu on a Windows window and select Details, you'll see the last date and time you modified the files in that window.

View menu and select Details. You can then see the last time and date you modified the folder or its contents. As Windows uses the time and date on your PC's clock to update this information, it's important to ensure that both are set accurately, otherwise the modified date will be useless to you. Windows gives you the power to do this using the Date/Time dialog box (see How to set the time and date, opposite).

● Putting the clock back

The Windows Date/Time dialog box also includes the option to adjust automatically for Daylight Saving Time. This is what the Americans call the system of putting the clocks forward in spring and back in autumn. If you leave this option switched on, Windows will automatically put your PC's clock backwards or forwards an hour on the right date.

The first time you switch on your computer after there has been a time change, Windows will warn you about the adjustment it's about to make and give you the chance to check that it's correct. It is important, therefore, to ensure that not only the time and date are correct but that your PC knows where it is in the world.

You don't have to alter the year on your PC – it happens automatically. Your computer has calendars programmed with all the dates up to 2099.

How to set the time and date

Here we show you how easy it is to set the date and time on your PC. We also show you how to set up or alter different time zones.

1 Like many other Windows settings, time and date can be managed from the Control Panel. Click on the Start button, choose Settings and then Control Panel. Double-click over the Date/Time icon to open the Date/Time Properties dialog box.

2 This is the dialog box for both the time and date. We want to change the month to September, so move the mouse pointer to the arrow on the right of the window with the month displayed (in this case, October). Click on the arrow, scroll down the menu and click on September.

FINDING DATED FILES

When you look at the contents of a folder with the Details option from the View menu, you'll see the time and date each file or folder was altered under the Modified heading.

This feature has hidden powers. For example, if you can't find a file on your hard disk, do a time search with the Find option in the Start menu (see Stage 2, pages 8-9).

3 To change the year, click on the up arrow by the year window to add one year at a time, or the down arrow to subtract a year. To change the day, click on the number of the day you wish to use in the main window.

4 Changing the time can be done by double-clicking on the hour (in this case 15) and entering the required hour. Move along to the minutes, double-click and change as required, then do the same for the seconds.

5 One thing to pay close attention to is the Current time zone, which is at the bottom of the window. In our example, it says Eastern Standard Time, which is fine if you live in New York, but most people don't. Click on the Time Zone tab to change this.

6 This is the Time Zone screen. Click on the arrow to the right of the current time zone and a long list of all the world's possible zones will appear (far right). Choose the one that suits your location by scrolling down the list (we've selected Greenwich Mean Time).

7 When all your time and date settings are correct, click OK to put them to work. As usual, there is an Apply option that allows us to see how the changes we made will affect the screen. Check that everything is correct and then press OK.

PC TIPS

Double-quick time

There are two quicker ways of reaching the Time/Date Properties dialog box than through the Control Panel. The first is to move your mouse pointer over the clock in the bottom right corner of the screen and double-click on it. Alternatively, you can move the mouse pointer over the clock, click with the right mouse button and then select Adjust Time/Date from the pop-up menu.

Software

Microsoft® Word

Microsoft® Excel

CorelDRAW™

Printing on envelopes

Now that you are using your word processor to create perfectly presented letters, why not complete the picture and give a great first impression by printing professional looking envelopes as well?

Y ou don't need any extra software, a special printer or computer-compatible stationery to have your envelopes printed by your PC. In fact, Word helps you produce them quickly and easily. You can even select the address from your finished letter and have Word place it in position on the envelope. Word will also print your own address (the return address) in the top left corner of the envelope, which looks neat and professional. Let's have a look at how easy it is to get Word to help you print great looking envelopes.

LET THE WIZARD HELP

You may find that it's fun to use Word's Envelope Wizard, which you'll find by going to the File menu, clicking New and selecting the Letters and faxes tab, then clicking on the Envelope Wizard.wiz icon (left).

The Wizard is useful if you need to print an envelope for something you didn't use Word to produce, but it is similar to Word's other method of producing envelopes (see opposite), where you highlight the address in a letter you have written. When using the Wizard, you don't have an address to copy, so you enter the recipient's address in one window, the return address in the window below and then click on Print. You have the same options that we feature opposite, as well as the paper clip icon (right) which you can click on for help.

● Creating an envelope

There are two methods of using Word to print envelopes. There is the Envelope Wizard (see left, 'Let The Wizard Help') or you may prefer to employ Word to do some of the work. You do this by going to the option in Word's Tools menu called Envelopes and Labels. With this method, Word copies the recipient's address straight from your letter and positions and prints it on to the envelope.

● Laying out your letter

We have already seen how to lay out a formal letter using Word (see Stage 1, pages 34-35). You place your address in the top right corner of the letter and the name and address of the person to whom you are sending it on the left, above the 'Dear …' line. All you have to do is highlight this name and address, so when you go to the Tools menu and click on Envelopes and Labels, the recipient's details are ready and waiting for you in the window that appears.

There are lots of different sizes and shapes of envelopes, but Word can handle anything you can fit into your printer and has ready-made templates for most common sizes.

You can produce such clear and well laid out letters that it would be a shame to send them in poorly presented envelopes.

Producing professional envelopes

Sending mail in clearly printed envelopes is a good idea for everyone, not just business people. Here's our guide to making that great first impression every time.

1 Here is our sample letter and, as you can see, the name and address of the person to whom the letter is being sent appears on the left of the page below the date.

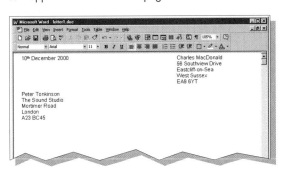

2 To let Word know the recipient's address, you highlight both the name and address. Do this by holding down the left mouse button at the start of the name and dragging the cursor to the end of the address. Then release the mouse button.

3 Now, move the mouse pointer to the Tools menu and select the Envelopes and Labels option.

4 You will see a dialog box displayed in the centre of your screen. The address you highlighted has been transferred to the Delivery address panel. The first time you do this, the bottom panel (the Return address box) may be empty. When you enter a Return address, Word remembers it and uses it in future letters.

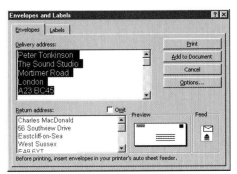

5 You need to check the size of your envelope. The standard size is 110 x 220mm (also known as DL). Click on Options in the Envelopes and Labels window and you'll see an Envelope size option (above right). It has a pull-down menu (right) with various envelope sizes. Click on the envelope size you want and then click OK.

PC TIPS

Add to Document

If you want to save a customized envelope with the document you designed it for, click on Add to Document in the Envelopes and Labels window. Word will then insert a new page at the start of your document in which it saves all the details.

6 Now let's reduce the size of the font for the return address to avoid confusion with the main address. In the Envelope Options window, click on Font under Return address and use the Size scroll bar to select a smaller font size. You can also change the font style by clicking any of the 11 Effects boxes. You can create shadows behind the address or have an outline drawn around it. Some of these effects could make life harder for the postman – so use them sparingly.

7 Some printers only accept envelopes fed into them in a certain way, but with most inkjet printers it is possible to have some say in the matter. Click the Printing Options tab in the Envelope Options window (above) to check the orientation of the envelope and which way up it goes into the printer (below left).

If the setup is correct, click on OK, which returns you to the Envelope Options window, and then click on Print (above right). You must ensure that your envelope is placed in the printer in the right way (see Stage 2, page 97 for guidance).

Putting text in columns

Whenever large amounts of information have to be presented in an easy-to-read format, or several different items need to appear near one another, you'll find text divided into columns.

Newspapers and magazines, for example, rely heavily on this format. Both need to display lengthy articles alongside shorter stories in a way that lets the readers find their way around the page with the minimum of fuss and confusion.

Since these columns are narrower than a single page (usually 70–100mm wide), you can scan the page and take in the information far more quickly than if the line extended to the full width of an A4 page.

With text spread over longer lines, readers risk losing their way; at least with columns, they know where they are.

● **When to use columns**
In Word you can easily format your documents into columns, although this will probably not be appropriate for all the documents you write. A single-page letter, for example, would look silly and confusing spread over two or more columns.

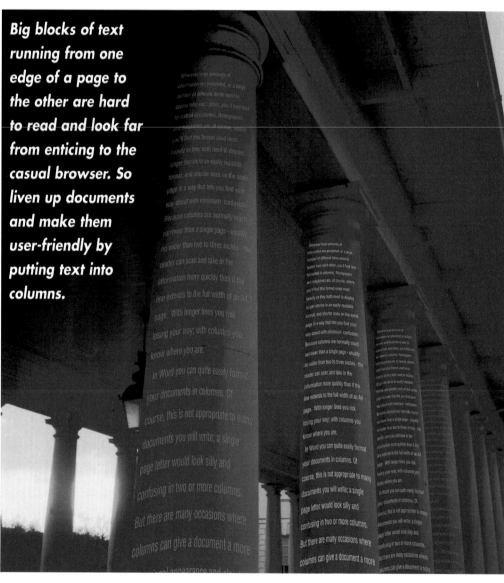

Big blocks of text running from one edge of a page to the other are hard to read and look far from enticing to the casual browser. So liven up documents and make them user-friendly by putting text into columns.

Structured columns of words are far more pleasing to the eye, and therefore easier to read, than large chunks of text that run from pillar to post.

However, there are many occasions when placing text into columns can give a document a more professional appearance. Business reports and club or society newsletters would all benefit from being put into a more accessible column format. We'll take an in-depth look at such documents on pages 30-33. For the time being, however, we'll concentrate on how to format a section of a longish document into columns.

EASY READING

It is quicker and easier to absorb large amounts of information when it is presented in short lines. When text is printed across a wide measure, the eye finds it hard to follow the story from one line to the next, and it becomes all too easy to lose your place on the page. For example, see how much easier it is to read the main text on this page, compared to the words in this box. Another big advantage of using columns of text is that they can be arranged around a picture if required and the reader will still have no difficulty in following the order. Pictures of any shape and size can be used without disrupting the flow of text. Notice the example in the picture above.

Formatting into columns

You can use any document with a reasonable amount of text for this exercise. Ideally, you need three or four pages to see the true benefits. If you don't have a longish document, simply copy and paste chunks of text to make up the length.

1 Highlight all the text that you wish to format into columns.

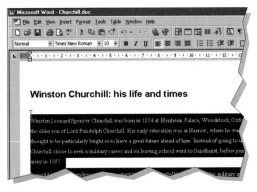

2 Go to the Format menu and select the Columns command.

3 The Columns dialog box now appears, as shown below.

4 At the top of the box are thumbnail images of a number of preset column styles. Click on them and you can see what they will look like in the Preview panel. The two right-hand images, labelled Left and Right give you the option of imposing unequal column widths, although these are very rarely used.

5 You can easily alter the column width and the space between the columns by clicking on the arrows next to the relevant figures to increase or decrease the measurements of column width or spacing. Word will automatically adjust the other measurement so that the total fits inside the page. Click on the up arrow to make a slight increase of 2mm in the space between the columns.

6 Above the Preview panel is a checkbox labelled Line between. If you click here to select it, Word will automatically draw a thin vertical line between the columns to emphasize the division between them.

7 Now press the OK button to see the columns in your document. The heading for our document is not affected by the Column command because we did not highlight it in Step 1.

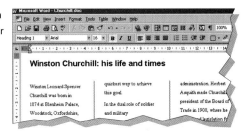

8 If you need to get an overall view of how these pages will look now that they are formatted in columns, select Full Screen view from the View menu. Now select a smaller percentage view – say, 50% – from the Zoom window at the top right of the toolbar.

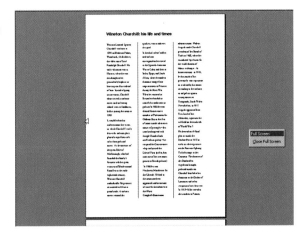

DISAPPEARING COLUMNS

You will notice that columns disappear from view when you select Normal from the View menu. This is because in Normal View, Word tries to display the document as quickly as possible. By using a single column on the left, it can show line breaks without taking time to draw all the columns.

Creating a newsletter

Newsletters for the local youth club or school PTA don't have to be dull, typed pages. Here we show you how to make your club look like it means business.

We've seen in Stages 1 and 2 how to change fonts and add pictures and, in the previous pages, how to use multiple columns to make large chunks of text more interesting. Now we are going to use all these tricks – and a few more – to create a newsletter.

Of course, not everyone needs to produce a newsletter. Yet it's amazing how the same principles – captioned pictures, headlines and box rules, for instance – can make a world of difference to many everyday Word documents. Homework essays and student dissertations, CVs and even basic memos or lists to be pinned up on a noticeboard can all be enhanced with these simple tricks.

● **Make your own**
It used to be the case that if you wanted to create anything livelier than the most basic document, you would use your word processor only to input and check the text, then transfer the words to an expensive and complex desktop publishing package to create the finished article. But, with a modern version of Word, you can achieve impressive results in one program, so saving yourself a good deal of time and money in the process.

You could even create something similar to *PCs Made Easy* in Word. All you have to do is get to grips with the necessary tools and you're in the publishing business!

The newsletter we're going to create is based on a Word Wizard-created document – but don't be afraid to experiment as it would be a very dull world if every publication had the same design.

Finally, an important design tip: don't be afraid to borrow ideas from the pros. Flick through magazines and choose the design features you like. Mix these ideas to create your own newsletters. It may sound like cutting corners, but it will save you several years at design school!

PC TIPS

If you are producing a newsletter, there can be a strong temptation to pack the page with as much as possible. Resist this desire and give yourself generous margins and plenty of space between different elements. Designers call these areas 'white space'.

Look at a selection of professionally designed newsletters and magazines and see how white space is used as effectively as any other element of a design.

As a designer would say, 'let the page breathe'. Space looks more attractive than clutter.

Hold the front page! Create your own news with Word's Newsletter Wizard.

Adding floating text boxes

Once you start using text boxes in more adventurous layouts, you'll discover just how versatile they can be.

THE KEY TO any newsletter layout is using boxes for the different elements, particularly text. It gives you the flexibility to create columns of text that flow between different parts of the page.

You need only link two text boxes together: when one box is full, the excess text flows over to continue into the next box.

You can change the size of the boxes at any time, and you can easily move them around until you get a balance that you like. When you alter the size or shape of the boxes the text automatically reflows. As text boxes are the most important elements of any newsletter-type layout, we'll show you how to use them in your Word documents.

Microsoft® Word

FLOATING BOXES

All boxes, including those we are adding in the exercise on this page, 'float' on top of the normal Word page. The space where you would normally type text sits underneath these boxes.

If you type without selecting one of the text boxes, the new text will appear at the current cursor position in the underlying Word text. If your document is blank (as it is here, underneath the text boxes), this text will appear at the top left of the page.

1 The text box tool is part of Word's drawing tools, so click on the Drawing button on the toolbar. When you do so, Word changes from Normal View to Page Layout View.

2 The view can change so that the whole page is visible on the screen. This is usually a 40 per cent view. To see more detail, ensure that the view is set to 100 per cent.

3 Click on the Text Box icon on the Drawing toolbar. It's in the centre of the toolbar below.

4 Now click and drag the mouse to create a rectangular text box on the Word page.

5 Click on the new text box, and type in a paragraph or two of text. To produce enough for this exercise, cut and paste it several times within the box until the text overflows the end of the box.

6 Now create a second text box, to the right of the first, by using the text box tool as you did in step 4.

7 Click on the first text box to select it, then click on the chain icon on the Text Box toolbar. You will see the cursor change into a jug icon.

8 Move your cursor over the second (empty) text box – it will change into a pouring jug – and click. The text will then overflow from the first box to the second.

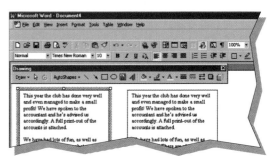

Using the Newsletter Wizard

Let's look at how we would go about creating a newsletter for a local football team. Word helps us make a start by providing the Newsletter Wizard.

1 Create a new Word document by selecting New from the File menu. The New dialog box will appear.

2 Now click on the Other Documents tab and double-click on the Newsletter Wizard icon.

3 When the Newsletter Wizard has started up, displaying the screen below, click Next.

4 The flow chart on the left of the window will show that you have moved to the next stage, where you are presented with a choice of three styles of newsletter: Professional, Contemporary and Elegant. We're using Professional because it is the most straightforward in design and the easiest to use. Leave the other settings exactly as they are and click Next.

5 The next screen lets us type in the name of our newsletter, 'Up the Park', and add a date and issue number. You can either accept Word's suggestions or type in your own. If you don't want any details at all, click on the tick boxes to remove the ticks. Then click Next.

6 The following screen allows you to print mailing labels. Click No, as our newsletters are going to be handed out at the ground. Then click Next.

7 The final screen will tell you that the Newsletter Wizard has everything it needs. Press the Finish button.

8 Word will create a newsletter with your title at the top, plus lots of dummy elements for holding text and pictures. At present, the boxes hold instructive dummy text. On the next page, we'll swap these dummy elements for our club newsletter information. But first check the paper size and change it if necessary (see PC Tips, below).

PC TIPS

The Newsletter Wizard creates documents based on US letter-sized paper. If you are using another size, such as European A4, you might have problems printing it. To change the page size, click on the File menu and select Page Setup. Click on the Paper Size tab and change from US Letter to A4. Click Apply to: whole document and then click OK.

A4 210 x 297 mm
A4 210 x 297 mm
Letter 8 1/2 x 11 in
al 8 1/2 x 14 in

Customizing your newsletter

The Newsletter Wizard does a lot of the work for you as it has the pages already laid out – all you have to do is insert text over what's currently there.

ONCE WORD has created your basic newsletter with dummy text and pictures, it's a good idea to print it out. This will give you a ready reference for the layout – just in case you accidentally delete something you may want later. What's more, the text on the page is a handy reference guide to creating the different items used and a breakdown of all the preset customized text styles, such as headlines, body text and quotes. There are two ways of adding and formatting your own text in the newsletter. You can either select and delete the document text, paste in your own and then format it afterwards, or you can change it bit by bit so that it keeps the styles already applied. The second method gives you more control and is suitable for creating text from scratch.

1 Replace the dummy text in the newsletter by simply highlighting it and typing over it. You can select complete paragraphs by triple-clicking (three rapid clicks of the left mouse button).

2 You could just replace all the text in the newsletter, but we want to jazz up a few of the headings as well. Highlight the heading in the first column and type in a new one. Then, from the Format menu, select Font. Choose a suitable font, size and colour and check how it will appear in the Preview panel. Be careful not to make the font too big, however, as it will unbalance the page.

3 Once you are happy with the heading style you have chosen, go to the Styles pull-down menu (with the heading still highlighted) and select Heading 1 – Professional, which is the preset style for this kind of heading.

4 Word knows that you have changed the font of one of the headings, and asks you whether you want to modify the other headings to match the change. Choose Update the style to reflect recent changes? and Automatically update the style from now on, then click OK. You will see other headings that use the same style automatically change to match the one you changed in Step 2.

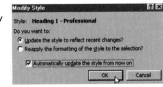

5 Now we're going to insert a picture. You could do this by selecting Picture from the Insert menu but as there is a picture already on the page, click on that and then select Insert Picture from the pop-up Picture toolbar.

6 Choose a picture – we found this example on the Microsoft Office CD–ROM. It's called 1stplace.wmf and appears in the Clipart folder.

7 The size of the picture is not quite right for our newsletter, but we can resize and trim it to fit. Click on the Crop button on the Picture toolbar and then click on one of the picture handles and move it in. Repeat this until you are satisfied. If you want to move the picture to a different point in the text, use Cut and Paste.

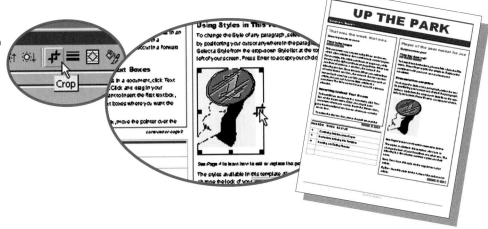

Talking tabs

The [Tab] key is useful for moving text across the page, but it can be customized to do so much more. Set up as many invisible stops as you wish, wherever you want, to create professional lists and documents.

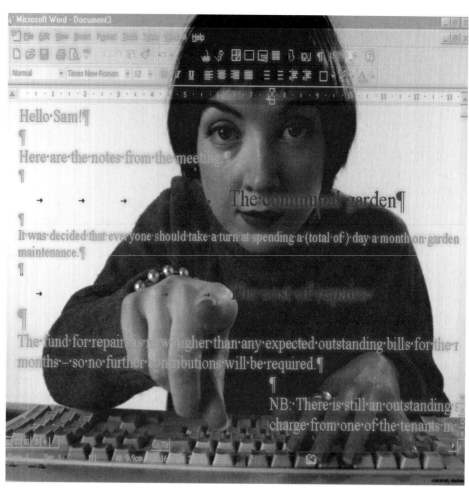

I n an earlier example (see Stage 1, pages 32-33) we used the [Tab] key in Word to make some simple indents in a letter. By pressing the [Tab] key several times at the beginning of each line of our address, we moved it to the right of our page to create a very simple letterhead layout.

Using tabs could be limited to just that, or they might simply be used for indenting the first line of each paragraph to make a letter look more presentable. However, tabs are far more versatile than that. They have many other easy-to-use applications which can be utilized on a wide variety of documents.

● Tab behaviour

If you press the [Tab] key when the text insertion point is at the beginning of a line of text, Word shifts the text to the right. Try it again on another line of text and you will see that Word shifts the text by exactly the same amount. Press it again and your second line of text will be indented to twice the distance of the first.

Now try typing the following on a blank line: 1 [Tab] 2 [Tab] 3 [Tab] Four [Tab] 5. You will notice that Word doesn't space the entries evenly – the distance between the 'r' of the word 'Four' and the number '5'

The [Tab] key will enable you to place words exactly where you want them on the page, making lists and documents neater and easier to read.

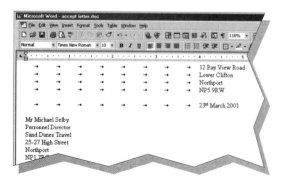

Here you can see the dozens of tabs we've had to use to move our address to the right of our letterhead. Once you've mastered tabs, you can do this with a single tab for each line.

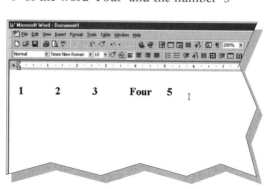

Despite initial appearances, tabs don't actually add any space. Instead they just shift text to the next invisible tab stop on the page; that's why the 'Four' appears to be closer to the '5' than the '3'.

is shorter than between the '1' and the '2'. This demonstrates an important facet of tabs: a tab doesn't actually add space; instead, Word shifts text to the next of a series of invisible tab stops (which are placed at half-inch intervals – roughly 1.3cm).

MEASUREMENTS

When setting tab stops or working with Word's ruler, you might have a preference for either centimetres or inches. Fortunately, Word lets you switch between these units as often as you like.

Click on the Tools menu and select Options. You will see a dialog box. Click on the General tab and at the bottom of the dialog box a drop-down list box will appear.

Select whichever measurement unit you want to use and then press the OK button. You will usually need to use only Centimeters and Inches. The Picas and Points options are measurements that are used in the publishing and printing industries.

● Changing settings
While these default tab stops are usually fine, there might be times when you require different settings. For example, Word can normally fit only 11 tab stops on an A4 page. Therefore, if you ever wanted to line up 12 columns of text, you would run out of space. To overcome this kind of problem, Word lets you specify both the position and number of tab stops.

● Alignment options
There's another way in which Word's normal behaviour might not be quite right for creating neatly aligned tables of information in your documents. If you press the [Tab] key to move to the next tab stop in a document, Word will align the text so that it starts at the tab. This is called left alignment. Type more text and you'll find it starts at the tab stop. As usual, this is the default – because it is the most popular choice. However, you may want to align your text differently and Word places other useful options at your disposal, such as creating special tab stops that help align each piece of text in subtly different ways.

For example, if you were creating a price list, you might use a tab to separate the item name and its price. Normally the table would look like this:

New engine	**£695.00**
Air filter	**£5.99**
Oil filter	**£17.95**

However, it's not clear at first glance that there's a big difference between the prices of these three components. It's a lot easier to see the difference when they are aligned on the decimal point:

New engine	**£695.00**
Air filter	**£5.99**
Oil filter	**£17.95**

Now it's easy to see the prices in relation to each other. By using a special decimal tab stop, you can get Word to line up information just like this. There are also right and centre tab stop options that can help to clarify the entries in other tables.

● Professional results
Other options can help make your tables of information look really smart. Most contents pages of books and magazines lay out the list of chapters or articles with their title, a tab and a page number. However, to make it easier to read across a wide column, the designer will often fill the space between the titles and page numbers with a continuous line of full stops.

Word lets you achieve the same results through its tab options. If you're creating a newsletter (see pages 30-33), adding a contents list as described above can help give it a polished and professional look.

● Following the rules
Adjusting the tab stops and choosing different alignment options is a very simple matter. By using the ruler (located just under Word's toolbars) you can add and remove any kind of tab stop with a few clicks.

You can also use the Tab's dialog box to add lines of full stops, or any other characters, to your contents lists. On the following pages we'll show you how to do all of this.

PC TIPS

You don't have to use tabs to indent the first line of paragraphs in your documents. If you want every paragraph to have an indented first line, you can save yourself time and trouble by applying this command as a default setting. Start with a new Word document and, before typing any text, click on the Format menu. Choose the Paragraph command and select the Indents and Spacing tab from the dialog box that appears.

Find the Special box on the right-hand side and choose First line from the options. Use the By number box to choose the amount of indent that you need, and then click OK.

As you type, you'll find that the first line of each paragraph is indented. However, if you want to apply indents to individual paragraphs, click the text insertion point in the paragraph you want before choosing the Paragraph command from the Format menu, as above.

Setting tabs using the ruler

The simplest way to add, change and remove tabs is to use Word's ruler. With a few clicks you can align your text and see the effects immediately.

1 We've started with a simple DIY shopping list as an example of something that would look better with the item name and price in two columns. If we used Word's normal tab stops, we'd have to use a different number of tabs for each line, depending on the text length of each item. For example, we'd need just one for the long 'Nails, screws, tacks' item, but several for the short 'Paint' item.

2 However, it's possible to do all this with one tab. Start by using the Select All command on the Edit menu.

3 Now that all the text is selected, we can apply our tab settings to it. Move the mouse pointer over the ruler. When you're roughly in the position you'd like your tab to be, click and hold down the mouse button.

4 A dotted line will show you the position of your new tab stop. Move it left or right and, when it is in the desired position, release the mouse button. Word will indicate your tab stop with a small L-shape on the ruler.

5 Click once again to remove the highlighting. Now click just in front of the price for the first item in the list ('3 tubes carpet glue'). Press the [Tab] key once and you will see the price move to the right, aligning its left edge directly under the tab stop.

6 Now do the same with the other prices. Only one tab will be needed each time.

7 The table looks OK, but it would be even better if the prices lined up on their decimal points. Start by selecting all the text again. Now remove the tab stop we put in by clicking on its L-shape on the ruler and dragging it onto the document; as you do, it will change from black to grey. Release it and it will disappear. The prices in the table will move and appear even more ragged than they did before, but don't panic – we'll soon fix that.

8 Change your style of tab stop by clicking on the square on the ruler's left side. Each time you click, it changes: left, right, centre, decimal and then back to left again. Click on it until the Decimal Tab is displayed.

9 Now, making sure that all the text in the document is still selected, move the mouse pointer to the position on the ruler where you placed the first tab. Click the mouse to position the decimal tab in the same place.

10 When you release the mouse button, the prices in the table will immediately realign from their ragged state. Word looks at the items and positions them so that their decimal points lie directly below the decimal tab stop.

MIXING YOUR TABS WITH WORD'S TABS

If you had already used tabs to format your list or table – with Word's normal half-inch tab stops – you will probably find that there are now too many tabs in your table. With Word's normal tab stops you often have to add several tabs to make things line up. Now, your single tab does the job, but any extra tab characters in the table make it look ragged. You can delete unwanted tab characters one by one until the table lines up under your own tab stop. To see the tab characters, click on the Show/Hide button on the Toolbar (right).

Fine-tuning your tab settings

Now we have worked with tab settings, let's make some changes to improve the look of the document we created in the previous exercise.

PC TIPS

You don't have to set tabs for the whole document all at once. In fact, if you have several different types of table in one document, you'll often have to fine-tune tab stops for each table.

You can set tabs for a single paragraph or line of text simply by selecting it before you use the ruler or Tabs dialog box, and then adding, moving or deleting the tabs.

1 You can create and alter tabs via the Tabs window in the Format menu. This has all the options of the ruler – and more besides. Start with a new Word document. Click on the Format menu and choose the Tabs command.

2 A dialog box will appear. At the top you will see a box which you can use to change the Default tab stops. As you can see here, Word is set to 1.27cm (half-inch).

3 You set tabs by typing a figure into the Tab stop position box. Type 5cm into the space provided and press the Set button below.

4 You'll see this tab stop position appear in the box just underneath. You can add more tab stops by repeating Step 3. As you press the Set button, each tab position appears in the list.

5 Deleting a tab stop is simple. Just highlight it in the list, then press the Clear button. Clear all the extra tabs until you have only the 5cm tab remaining.

6 You can also select the type of alignment for each tab stop in the Alignment section. Highlight the 5cm tab stop and you'll see that the Left alignment option is selected. Select another option and press the Set button. Here, we've chosen Decimal.

7 The other section of the dialog box is called Leader, and it's here that you can tell Word to fill in the space between tabs with characters. There are four options, the second one of which uses full stops and is often seen in contents and price listings. When you add a tab stop, Word doesn't normally use leader characters: the '1 None' option is selected by default. Select our 5cm tab stop and then click on the full stop option. Press the Set button.

8 We can apply this new tab trick to the DIY listing that we made on the previous page. When you have finished that exercise, select all the text by clicking on Select All in the Edit menu. Go to the Tabs box and clear the tab you set previously, as we did in Step 5. Change the tab stop settings by adding a Decimal aligned tab at 5cm and selecting the second option from the Leader options. Press the Set button and then press the OK button. You'll now see a neat and easy-to-read list.

Items needed for renovation of lounge

3 tubes carpet glue......................£3.75
Contiboard................................£18.75
Beech planks..........................£117.89
Paint stripper.............................£3.49
Nails, screws, tacks....................£6.50
Paint......................................£25.75

Total.....................................£176.13

Inserting special characters in text

Word doesn't limit you to just ordinary letters and numbers in your text documents. You can also add foreign characters and a whole range of useful symbols and icons to create the right effect for your intended message.

One of the advantages of a personal computer over a typewriter is that it allows you to use all sorts of extra characters as well as the ordinary alphabet letters and numbers. This makes it as easy to produce an informal letter, adorned with little doodles and pictures, as it does to write a letter in a foreign language with accents, or a business letter with symbols.

Most of these special characters don't appear on your computer keyboard, apart from the punctuation and currency symbols. But, by using special commands, Word puts as many as 200 different characters at your disposal – and even more can be added with extra fonts.

● Improving letters and documents

This versatility gives you the ability to produce documents with a professional finish or with a large element of fun and frivolity.

Special characters can be divided into three main categories: foreign characters (such as ç or é); business symbols (such as © or ™); and fun symbols (♥ or ✗). There are two ways to insert these characters. The first is to pick them out from a grid, via the Symbol command on the Insert menu. Some characters can also be entered using the keyboard. This is done by pressing a combination of keys.

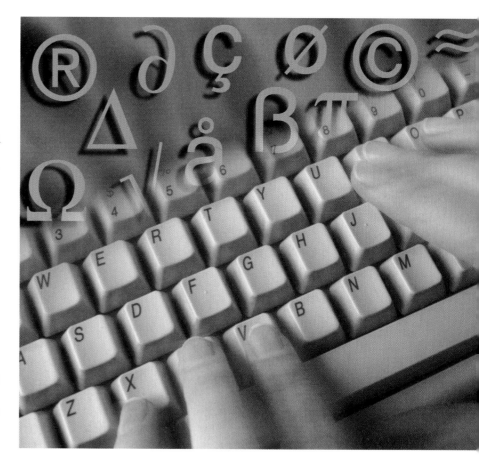

Your keyboard can contain up to 200 hidden characters and symbols – all you have to do is find them!

Although this method is quicker if you use foreign characters a lot, it is more complicated.

It's easy to see how different types of letters and documents can benefit from these additions. A foreign-language letter, for example, would be impossible to write correctly without these characters. Equally, business letters can be made to look more professional if you use ready-made symbols, such as those for copyright or trademark. Fun symbols may not be as important, but they can pep-up a letter or party invitation.

Adding symbols

Use foreign characters and fun symbols to enhance your letter-writing.

TO ILLUSTRATE HOW special characters can be both useful and fun, we'll write a love letter to an absent girlfriend. Here is an example using both accented characters and symbols:

My Dear Gisèle,

Was it only yesterday we said goodbye? Je pense à toi. Les feuilles mortes sont tombées des arbres, mais mon amour reste toujours vivant. Ça me soulage que tu reçoive ma lettre. Je serai encore une fois avec toi, ô mon trésor éternel.

❤ Je t'embrasse ❤

Christian ✗✗✗✗✗ ☺

1 Type in the text until you reach a special character. Then select the Insert menu and choose Symbol.

Microsoft® Word

2 When the Symbol window opens, select the Symbols tab and choose (normal text) from the Font drop-down menu.

3 Now look at the grid and select the character you are looking for, in this case è, by clicking on it with the left mouse button. A large version of the character will be displayed on a blue background. When you click on the Insert button, the character will appear in the text document (inset).

4 Close the Symbol window and carry on through the letter, entering all the letters with accents in the same way. The next special character is the heart symbol. This is entered in a similar way, but is part of the Symbol font, so select Symbol from the Font drop-down menu.

My Dear Gisè

5 Click on the heart in the Symbol characters grid, then click on the Insert button. When you come to insert the second heart, save time by copying and pasting the first one. Have a look at all the symbols in this grid to see the variety available for use in different types of document.

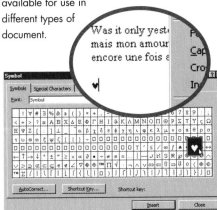

6 If you want to add other embellishments, try an '✗' for kisses after the signature. This is part of the Wingdings font, so select this font and choose from the grid as before. Again, you don't need to insert each '✗' separately, just copy and paste the first one.

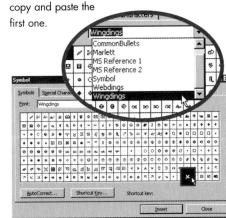

7 Another symbol is the 'smiley' face. This is also one of the Wingdings font characters. Insert this at the end of the document. All the special characters appear in the font size you are using to write your letter, but this time, let's make it bigger. You do this in exactly the same way as with an ordinary character. Select the 'smiley' and put up the font size to 48.

Finding and replacing text

Are you looking for a quick way to get to the right part of your document, to add some formatting to frequently occurring words or to correct a name misspelled throughout it? If so, Word's powerful find and replace tool is what you need. It will even search for 'sound-alike' words.

It can sometimes be difficult to find exactly the part of a Word document that you want to work on, especially if it is a long document. The most obvious, but cumbersome, way is to scroll right through the document until you find what you're looking for. However, Word provides a much more flexible way of dealing with this.

Word includes a Find tool that allows you to search for occurrences of words or phrases within your document. This means you only have to remember a relevant word from the part of the document you want to work on, then you can use the Find tool to skip through the places that word occurs in the document until you reach the one you want. This tool can also be handy when you want to find certain key words or phrases in documents with which you are unfamiliar.

● **Changing words and phrases**
Word's Find tool is not just a search tool for locating words and phrases – you can also use it to replace them with different words or phrases. For instance, you could replace all the occurrences in a document of British Broadcasting Corporation with BBC in one swift operation. Or you could correct all the occurrences of somebody's name if you discover that you've spelt it incorrectly.

In fact, it's not just words and phrases you can replace – you can actually replace any sequence of characters. For instance, many typists were originally taught to add two spaces after the full stop. If this is a habit you just can't break, you can search for two consecutive spaces and replace them with one.

There are also other special characters that you can replace, such as paragraph marks, tab characters and page breaks. The Word find and replace tool has some other advanced features. For example, if you're not sure of the spelling of a word you need to look for, you can ask Word to search for a word that sounds like the one you type in. You can also get the Find and Replace tool to look for words that appear in a particular format (for example, typeface, size, bold, italics and so on). You can instruct Word to replace these words with different words in the same format or the same words in another format.

Word also lets you match case. This means that if you want to replace the name of a company called 'FAST', but leave the ordinary word 'fast' as it is, Word can oblige.

Using Word's find and replace tool

The Find and Replace tool helps you locate and replace any sequence of text, including numbers and special characters. It makes it easy to move around long documents and change misspelt words in a single action.

1 Here's a letter that we've been working on. There's a mistake in one of the names – the first George Smith should be Andrew Smith. Let's use Word's find and replace tool to put things right.

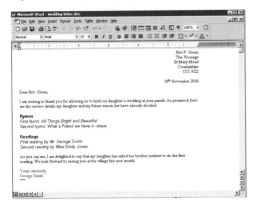

2 Position the text cursor at the start of the letter so that Word will search through the whole document from the beginning. Now select Replace from the Edit menu.

3 The Find and Replace dialog box appears: type the word George in the Find what text box at the top of the dialog box. Then type in the word Andrew in the Replace with text box. If we wanted to change all the occurrences of the name George to Andrew, we would just press the Replace All button. However, we won't do this here because we want to show more advanced replace options.

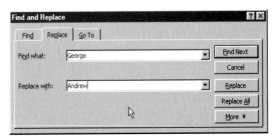

4 Let's exploit the difference in format between the two occurrences of the name George (one is in italics, the other is not). Click on the More button and the Find and Replace dialog box will extend to reveal more options. Click once in the Find what text box, then click over the Format button and choose the Font option.

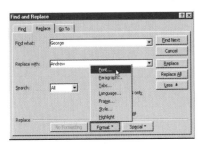

5 Use this dialog box to specify the format of the word to replace. We chose 10pt Arial with an italic style (to find George in italics). Select suitable settings for your document and click on the OK button.

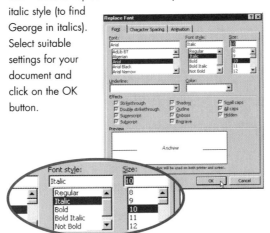

6 Position the cursor in the Replace with text box, click on the Format button and select Font again. Repeat the choices we made in Step 5 and click OK. Notice how both text boxes have identical Format lines below them.

7 Click on the Replace button and Word will locate all words in the style specified in Step 5 and ask you to confirm each replacement as you go. For this exercise, click on the Replace All button. Word makes all the replacements (one in this case) and reports back to you. Click on the OK button in the dialog box that reports the number of changes (below).

8 Click on the Close button in the Find and Replace dialog box and you'll see your modified document with only the one George changed to Andrew, as intended.

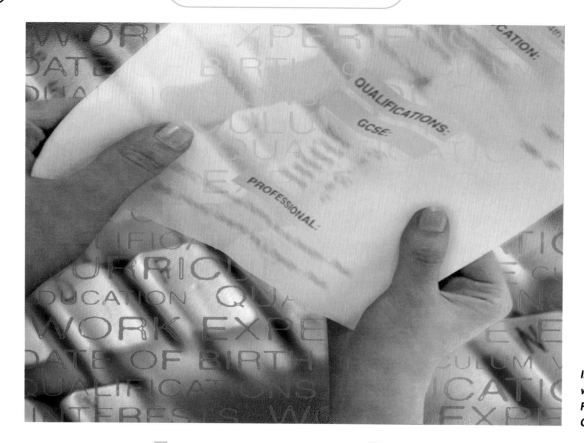

If you're applying for a job, why not take advantage of your PC's capabilities to make your CV look as good as possible?

Borders and shading

Adding borders and highlights to give your curriculum vitae a really professional look couldn't be easier when you're using Word.

If there is one document you just have to have professionally presented, it is your CV – your curriculum vitae or life history. The CV is the document that clinches an interview for a job or college place – or ruins your chances – and it is absolutely vital that it creates the right impression.

● The computer advantage
All too many CVs are simply typed out in a haphazard way or, worse still, handwritten. With a PC and a printer, however, you have at your fingertips the power to produce a clean, neat document that will make the most of your chances. Even better, by spending a little time making your CV as clear, concise and attractive as you can, you will increase the chances that yours will stand out from the rest of the pile and help get you that interview and, ultimately, the job.

With a PC, it is easy to make last-minute corrections to your CV to ensure every detail is right. You can also update it to incorporate your most recent work experience or each new qualification – no more handwritten corrections that make your CV look scruffy. You can modify it, too, to suit the different types of job that you may want to apply for. And, perhaps most importantly of all, you have complete control over the way it looks.

Over the next few pages, we give you a few tips on preparing a CV. In particular, we'll show you how to use Microsoft Word's tools to create a really professional look – adding borders and shading to emphasize specific features to draw the eye to important sections.

It is vital with a CV to present everything in clear, easy-to-understand sections so that the

CHECKPOINT

MAKING THE MOST OF YOUR CV

As well as the formatting ideas covered in the step-by-step examples (see pages 44-45), there are a few general principles to consider when creating a CV. Follow the tips here and your CV is less likely to end up in the reject pile because of poor presentation.

☑ Try to avoid using capital letters and italics for large chunks of text. Both make your information harder to read than normal text.

☑ Avoid the temptation to use decorative typefaces. They might be fun for the odd letter or jokey poster, but most potential employers are looking for efficient, business-like employees.

☑ Be wary of using humour in your text – it's not what the CV is for.

☑ Always get your referees' permission to put their details on the CV. Neither they nor a potential employer will be impressed if you haven't.

☑ Keep your CV to a maximum of two A4 pages, unless you are specifically asked to do otherwise.

reader can see at a glance what your education was, what your recent employment history has been, and so on.

Borders are an excellent way of sectioning off different parts of your CV. They also make it look bolder and more interesting, and this can help make a rather lightweight CV look a little more substantial, without distorting the facts.

● Dividing your life up

You should always start your CV with your name, address and contact numbers (phone, fax, email and so on). Follow this with your date of birth, nationality (if relevant) and other background details. Some people prefer to put all this information in the centre of the page, using the centre text control. Others prefer it on the left of the page, which is known as ranged left text. The rest of the CV then divides into three main areas: education and qualifications, employment history and related experience. The idea

is to give the reader a clear outline of your life, so each entry in these three sections begins with the relevant dates. With the employment history, keep entries brief and to the point, but make sure it is clear what you were doing in each job, listing in order: dates, your job title, your employer's name and address and what your job entailed.

● The right order for you

Recruitment experts advise putting your employment history in reverse order. That means that you begin with the most recent jobs. Remember, when potential employers are reading through lots of CVs, they probably want to see what you're currently doing, without having to wade through your entire career of part-time, holiday and temporary jobs.

Others think that your employment history should be in chronological order down the page for absolute clarity. It is really up to you to decide which works best with your life history and also shows potential employers the important facts most clearly.

The final sections should cover your personal interests, which can be surprisingly helpful at getting you that interview, and the names and contact details of two referees who will give you good references. These are usually work-related, but some employers also like a personal referee.

WHEN TO USE UNDERLINE AND WHEN TO USE BORDERS

Most of the time you will use the Borders tool to add horizontal lines under some text in your documents. But you might also have been using Word's Underline tool (below) to achieve the same effect. Which one is better?

Underlining

In Word, you can emphasize any amount of text, from a single word to the whole document, by using the underline command, which places a single line under the text selected. Some people also use the Underline tool to add a horizontal rule across a page, by adding a whole

Once you've got used to adding borders, you'll probably only use Word's Underline button for adding a single underline to individual words and short phrases.

line of spaces, selecting them and then clicking on the Underline button. While this might look fine, it's a time-consuming approach. There are other potential problems, too: for example, if you increase the size of the text used in the document, you will find that the line of space overlaps onto another line – and so does the underline.

Borders

When you use borders for such lines, however, you'll find you have much more flexibility available at the press of a few buttons. For example, you have a wide choice of different line widths and you can choose from a variety of styles, including solid, dotted and even wavy lines. When you work with borders, you'll discover

that you can use them on any side of your text. You can put lines on one, two or three sides of the text, or even completely enclose it.

As you experiment with the borders options, you'll find that in most cases they're more suitable than the Underline tool. On the whole, while underlining is the best option for emphasizing a word or phrase in formal letters and documents, the borders options are much more suitable for making paragraphs or longer sections stand out.

Special effects, such as wavy lines and 3D edges, won't suit all of your documents, but they show the extra flexibility of Word's border options.

Adding borders to separate sections of your CV

To show you the basic steps of producing a CV, we've created an imaginary example for someone applying for the job of supermarket manager. You can either copy the format of this CV or create your own.

1 Type in the text of your CV, following the guidelines given (see Checkpoint box on the previous page). For the moment, don't add any formatting other than tabs to create columns. All the formatting commands will be added later on.

2 To divide the CV into clear sections, you can create lines across the page under each separate heading with the Borders and Shading option. Start by clicking on the line beneath Personal Details (or whatever your first heading is).

3 Now go to the Format menu at the top of the screen and pull down the menu. Select the Borders and Shading option and click on it to bring up the Borders and Shading window on the screen.

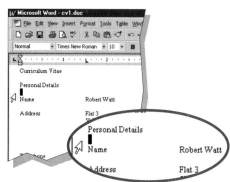

4 The Borders and Shading window shows a Preview, plus a choice of Style, including hatched, dotted and solid border options. We shall choose the default option, which is a simple solid line.

5 Click on the button which shows a top border and a line will appear across the top of the text in the preview panel. Click OK to put this in your CV.

Click on diagram below or use buttons to apply borders

6 The Personal Details section should begin with a neat line (inset). Now go through the rest of the document adding a border at the beginning of each section in turn – Education and Qualifications, Employment History, and so on.

PC TIPS

Spacing borders

When you add a border to a section of your text, you will see that Word leaves a standard distance between the text and the border. Usually this distance will look fine, but you might find that you need the border a little closer or further away from the text. In fact, Word lets you change the distance in any of four directions. First, open up the Borders and Shading window as before and click on the Options button in the bottom right-hand corner (top). Another window pops up with a number of options (right). In the From Text section, you will be able to set the distance you want the border to appear from your text, at the top, bottom

and both sides. The easiest way to adjust these settings is to click on the up and down arrows next to each figure (left).

Adding emphasis

Shading is a great way of making words stand out.

TO MAKE each of the section headings stand out clearly, you can use Word's shading option. One way to use this is to reverse the normal colours so that the headings are white text on a black background. For our fictitious CV, we want to make all the section headings, such as Personal Details, Education and Qualifications and Employment, stand out to make the CV easier to read.

1 Click just to the left of the heading you want to highlight, in this case, Personal Details. Choose Borders and Shading from the Format menu as you did for Borders (see page 44, Step 3).

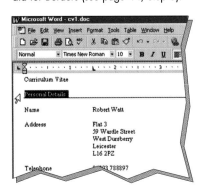

2 When the Borders and Shading window comes up on the screen, look for the Shading tab at the top of the window and click on it. This brings up a box with coloured squares in the Fill section.

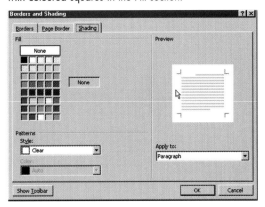

PC TIPS

Like many of the features in Word, you can also access most of the Border commands from the toolbar. Press the Outside Border button (right) and the current paragraph will be bordered or you can highlight the text you want to border and then press the button. Choose the border type you want by clicking the bar to the right of the Outside Border button and selecting your choice from the pop-up box (below, right).

3 The Fill section allows you to select the colour of the shading. This is white by default. To make it black, click on the black square. The Preview on the right will now change to black to show you the effect. If you like it, click on OK.

4 The whole line now goes black. To shade only the words, click on the Right Indent marker on the ruler and drag it to the left.

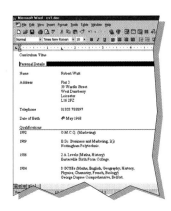

5 As you drag the Right Indent marker to the left, the dotted line shows the width. Release it when it corresponds with the inner margin.

6 To see the effect, click anywhere in the document. Notice that the line beneath the shading is visible again and the text is white on black.

7 Repeat the procedure outlined in Steps 1–6 for all the other section headings in your CV. To finish the document off, you could embellish the text by selecting an attractive, but business-like, typeface, such as Arial.

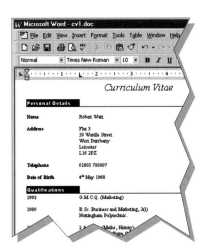

Using Word's drawing tools

If a picture paints a thousand words, then why not make the most of the possibilities offered by Word's drawing tools? Use them to liven up documents such as letters, CVs and newsletters.

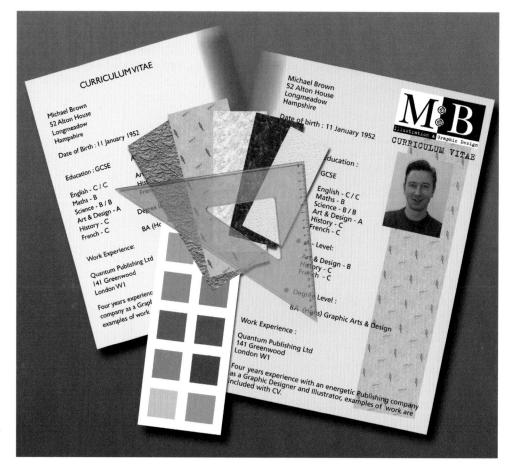

W e have already touched on how you can add photographs and illustrations to text (see Stage 1, pages 44-47). However, both of these exercises assume that you have access to the type of graphics you want to use. The examples we used were perfectly acceptable but when you want to do something specific, such as create a professional looking logo, they may not necessarily be a great deal of help. Not only will they probably not look quite right, but other Word users will recognize them for what they are straight away.

(to name just a few), will give you more than enough scope to create some highly impressive graphics, and it will be quicker than working with a completely separate graphics program.

Stand out from the crowd. Use Word's drawing tools to give documents a professional look.

● Better graphics

Fortunately, Word has a number of advanced tools with which you can create all manner of individual graphics. In fact, it not only has some of the fundamental tools of a drawing package, such as CorelDRAW, but also contains some rather clever and fun-to-use three-dimensional features.

Combining these tools with the basic options, such as coloured fills, coloured lines, patterned rules and customizable preset shapes

● Personalized portfolio

Another extremely useful facet is that all the graphics you create can be edited. This means that you can gather together a portfolio of graphics, each one of which is slightly different, to theme an extensive document or to make variations on your logo for use on letterheads or compliment slips.

This also allows you to come back to the designs whenever you like so you can create further variations as your needs change.

The drawing tools

Word has an impressive selection of tools hidden in its Drawing toolbar. When you know where to find them, your Word documents could take on a whole new shape.

THE DRAWING tools can be broken down into a few broad categories. There are buttons you can see on the Drawing toolbar, then tools and commands which are available through drop-down lists.

Look along the toolbar (shown below) and you'll see buttons that look, and work, like those in other packages: lines, arrows, rectangles and circles, plus line style and colour options. Using these could not be more straightforward. Simply click on the appropriate button, then move the mouse to the page and click and hold the mouse to

draw the object on the page. Other buttons allow you to change the colour of the objects and their outlines.

● For Word's next trick...

Word also has some tricks of its own, one of which is AutoShapes – shapes and lines that you draw in much the same way as the simple drawing tools but which have a built-in intelligence, which makes them very easy to customize to your exact requirements. Finally, there are shadow and 3D commands that you can apply to boxes on the page.

Microsoft® Word

Select Objects
Lets you select one or more objects

Free Rotate
Rotates any object with the mouse

Autoshapes
Adds Word's ready-made shapes

Line
Draws simple lines

Arrow
Draws arrows

Rectangle
Draws squares and rectangles

Oval
Draws circles and ellipses

Text Box
Adds a box for text

Draw
A drop-down list of advanced commands (see box below)

Insert WordArt
For special effects with text

Fill Colour
Fills an object with a solid colour

Line Colour
Specifies line and outline colour

Text Colour
Chooses a colour for text

Line Style
Chooses a thickness for lines

Dash Style
Specifies outline appearance

Arrow Style
Specifies arrow's appearance

Shadow
Adds a drop-shadow to an object

3D
Adds a 3D look to an object

ADVANCED DRAWING TOOLS AND OPTIONS IN THE TOOLBAR

The drop-down list of options in the toolbar's Draw menu is concerned with how the objects 'sit' on the page and how they relate to each other. The grouping options let you combine or separate objects. Group combines them; Ungroup breaks them up again.

The options under the Order menu let you move objects in front of, or behind, each other. Bring Forward and Send Back shift the object, one level at a time; Bring to Front or Send to Back moves the element to the front or to the back of an overlapping stack of objects.

Objects you draw usually float on top of the Word document you

are working on. However, the Send Behind Text command puts an object under the Word text. This is useful for adding a coloured panel behind the text.

Word usually helps you line up objects on the page when you draw or move them by snapping them to an invisible grid. Grid lets you turn this facility off if you want to line objects up by hand.

Nudge commands shift objects by tiny amounts. With the Align or Distribute commands you can get Word to position objects. You can choose whether to line them up or have them evenly separated. The Rotate or

Flip commands allow you to rotate an item by exact amounts or flip it to make a mirror image (you can do this horizontally or vertically). By using the Edit Points command you can subtly alter the shape of special AutoShapes, such as smooth curved lines.

Change AutoShape lets you change one AutoShape into another – a circle into a multi-pointed star, for example.

Set AutoShape Defaults allows you to customize a shape so it is exactly how you want it each time you draw it. For example, draw a square and change the thickness of its outline to 6pt. By clicking on Set AutoShape Defaults, any shape you subsequently draw will also have a 6pt border.

Drawing simple pictures in a letter

Word's drawing tools should not be underestimated. Not only are they powerful enough to enable you to be creative, but they are also available at the click of a mouse button.

1 Let's set up an imaginary example, adding some simple pictures to a letter explaining some work to be done on the garden. Once you've entered your letter text, click on the Drawing button on the toolbar.

2 Now select the Rectangle tool and draw a rectangle on the page. We'll use this as our garden outline. Unfortunately, the text of the letter runs under the rectangle.

3 Click on the rectangle with the right mouse button and select the Format AutoShape option from the menu that pops up.

4 Click on the Wrapping tab from the Format AutoShape dialog box that appears. Click on the Square option and then click the OK button. You will now see that the text wraps to create a new line, instead of disappearing under the rectangle.

5 Now we'll change the colour of the garden. Make sure the rectangle is selected, click on the Fill Color button and then select a suitable square from the drop-down palette. The rectangle will fill with your chosen colour. Now we want the green to look patchier, so that it reflects its poor state.

6 Click the Fill Color button and select Fill Effects. This dialog box lets you add many different types of effect. Click on the Pattern tab.

7 You'll see a variety of patterns. Choose one that looks a little patchy. Press the OK button and your rectangle will then change.

8 Now we want to add a shed using the same steps. Choose a roof colour and pattern.

9 We used the horizontal lines for our pattern, but now we want brown planks with white lines – not the other way round. To do this, bring up the Pattern tab of the Fill Effects dialog box (Steps 6 and 7) and switch the Foreground and Background colours. Press the OK button to see the effect on your garden shed.

10 We're going to finish our first plan by adding the paved walkway from the back of the house to the garden shed. Now we're ready to use Word's more advanced drawing tools to draw a diagram that will show how we want the garden to look (opposite).

Using advanced drawing tools

We can use some more of Word's drawing capabilities to finish the garden plan started on the opposite page. Here we'll show you how to add some fine details.

1 Start with the letter we created opposite. Use this to make a similar garden layout to which you need to add several small dark green circles (using the circle tool) to indicate small shrubs.

2 We want to add a special object that will draw the attention of our gardener to an area for a barbecue. Click on the AutoShapes button, select the Stars and Banners list and then click on the first shape: Explosion 1. Use the mouse to drag the shape to the top of the garden (inset right).

AUTO SHAPES

Word's basic shapes are easy to add to your documents, but there are times when you will need more complex shapes, which Word supplies. You can select one of these and then tweak it to form the exact outline you need.

Click on the AutoShapes button and you'll see that Word has six categories. For example, there are ready-made star shapes, arrow-heads and speech bubbles.

AutoShapes' Lines options are also very useful when you need more than straight lines. The Scribble tool lets you draw lines by hand and will follow the exact path your mouse takes on the mouse pad. Use the Curve tool to smooth the line or try the Freeform tool to combine Curve and Scribble.

3 Use the Fill Color palette to colour in the explosion shape. Make sure it's a shade that will be easily noticed to avoid it being confused with the other existing garden objects.

4 Now we'll use another of Word's AutoShapes to create an ornamental pond. Select the Moon shape from the Basic Shapes collection and drag the crescent into the blank area of the garden.

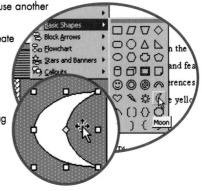

5 The Moon is a special kind of shape: there's an extra handle (the small yellow diamond) in addition to the usual handles along the edge. AutoShapes with these special handles can be tweaked. Click and drag this handle to the right.

6 This handle controls the curvature of the concave side of the Moon, making it more or less bowed (experiment with other AutoShapes to see other ways these diamond handles work).

7 Use the patterns tab of the Fill Effects dialog box to fill the pond. Choose suitable blue colours and the wavy lines option to represent the water surface.

8 Here we've added the final touches (right) – some more shrubs by the pond and a patio area. Use the rectangle and oval tools to add these. Such simple diagrams give you an idea of what you can achieve in a few minutes, without even firing up another graphics program.

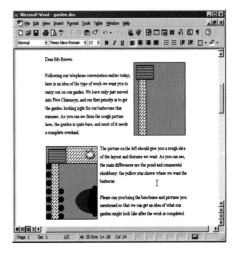

Using mail merge

Sending the same circular letter to a group of people can be extremely time-consuming as you have to personalize each one. Fortunately, Word can lend a helping hand, with a special feature called mail merge.

There are various occasions when you need to send similar letters to several people. Sometimes, a basic form letter will do. Often, however, although most of the text can remain the same, it is much better if each letter is personalized. For example, party invitations or speculative letters to potential employers look much better when they are individually addressed.

● Changing information
You can amend each letter by hand but Word's mail merge facility makes the job much easier. With mail merge you need only write the document once and then tell Word what you want changed, so you can print hundreds of personalized letters with a single operation.

The principle behind mail merging is that you store the parts of a letter that change (such as the name, address, and so forth) in a separate database. This information can then be incorporated into a letter (or other document) in positions that you specify. All you need to do is create the basic letter, inserting special codewords in the places where you want the variable information to be inserted from the database, and then bring the two together.

You've probably seen examples of 'junk mail' created this way. Such letters usually set the data up in another program, which is one reason you sometimes see letters addressed to 'Dear Mr 10 Park Rd'. Thankfully, Word makes everything far simpler.

This is partly because you do everything in one program, although Word still creates two documents: a form letter and a data source. It also has an easy-to-follow dialog box – called the Mail Merge Helper – to take you through the whole process in detail.

● A simple example
For our first step-by-step exercise, we are going to take the example of a school circular to tell parents about the forthcoming sports day. This is a very simple mail merge and only requires basic data to be entered. But even this example illustrates another advantage of mail merging. If you want to send another letter to the same people – providing the sports day

Professional, personalized and relatively painless...mail merge can save you time and effort.

Microsoft® Word

results, perhaps – you can re-use the names and addresses from the database without having to retype them.

● **Setting up mailing data**

Although this example uses only simple data to create a brief letter, the same principles apply no matter how complicated the data or how long the Word documents are that you want to generate. All you have to do is insert meaningful markers, or fields, in the document that correspond to the entries in your database.

You can have as many fields as you like. You can even sort or filter the mailing according to the data that appears in them. In our first example, we want everyone on the list to get the same letter. But in the second example (see page 53), we will see how to use more

advanced options to ensure that only members of the PTA council get a letter.

Mail merges can be as complex as you want, depending on the details in the database. For instance, when mailing a club membership, you could include information on whether or not a subscription has been renewed and so write only to those who haven't paid up!

The mail merge facility is so efficient that it can incorporate many different types of variable information in the same document. For example, a self-employed home PC user could use a database of customers and create different sets of letters for good customers and late payers on a monthly basis.

When you start mail merging you go straight into setting up your database, but don't feel nervous – there is lots of hand-holding to ensure quick results.

WHAT IT MEANS

FIELDS

In a mail merge document, a field is a block of data that is held in a database. When you are preparing a mail merge, Word automatically sets up your data in separate fields that might include entries for, say: title (Mr, Miss, Dr, etc); first name; surname; first line of address (house number and street name); second line of address (district); city; postcode; and country.

Word also uses fields as special place markers in a document. These fields indicate places that are reserved for information, which Word automatically adds, eg a field can automatically insert current date or time.

In the case of a mail merge, when you prepare the letter for merging you can include fields that correspond to the blocks of data in your database. The fields in the letter can then draw upon the data and place the correct details in the document when you complete your merge.

Creating data for your mail merge

The mail merge process is divided into two main parts; creating fields to use in your mail merge and adding the fields to the letter or document you want to merge.

1 Start with a new blank Word document, then select the Mail Merge command from the Tools menu.

2 The Mail Merge Helper appears. Click on the Create button and select Form Letters from the pop-up menu (top right). A dialog box pops up asking which document to use (below right). Click Active Window.

3 Now we will start creating a database to hold the parents' information, such as names and addresses. Click the Get Data button and then select the Create Data Source option.

4 You will now see a dialog box that helps you create the fields for your mail merge letter. Word suggests many different types of fields in a list on the right-hand side. For our mailshot to parents, we don't need all the fields on offer.

You can delete irrelevant fields by clicking on them and then pressing the Remove Field Name button (below left). Change the list so that it reads: Title, FirstName, LastName, Address1, Address2, City and PostalCode (below right). Then press the OK button.

5 Before you can add names and addresses of parents to your mail merge database, you will be prompted to save it. Use the Save As dialog box to locate a suitable folder (we've used a folder called My Files), then give the file a name and save it.

6 Word now lets you know that your mail merge database (the data source) is still empty. It gives you a choice of adding names and addresses by clicking the Edit Data Source button or writing your mail merge letter by clicking on the Edit Main Document button.

We'll add the names and addresses first, so click the Edit Data Source button.

7 You now see the Data Form dialog box. This looks like an index card in which you add parents' details one at a time by typing into the boxes next to the field names you set up. Fill in dummy entries for the first person, then click Add New to add another set of details. The Record box (bottom left) shows how many people you have entered. Repeat until you have three or four examples, then press the OK button to create your letter.

Creating a merge letter

1 After Step 7 (above) the first thing to notice as you switch back to your letter document is the special mail merge toolbar (see below). This is used to enter the merge fields, which, for this example, will all be located at the top of the letter (right), where you'd normally put the recipient's name and address.

2 At the top of the document, place the mouse in the position where you want to add the first field (the Title). Press the Insert Merge Field button. A drop-down list of fields appears. Select Title. The word Title will appear in the document between special markers to show that it is a field (inset).

3 Continue adding fields until the letter looks like the one shown. If you are writing to people you know well, you could use FirstName. Note that wherever you have two fields next to one another, you must put spaces between them (inset) or the data will print with no spaces.

4 Now type the rest of your letter as usual, making up a few lines about the sports day. When you finish, save it as Sports letter and select the Mail Merge Helper from the Tools menu (above). When the dialog box (right) pops up, click the Merge button to start merging the data with the letter.

5 Now the Merge dialog box pops up. Leave the settings as they are and click the Merge button. Word now inserts the data into the letter to create a new document, with one page for each person typed into the Data Form dialog box (inset).

PRINTING MAIL MERGES

In Step 5 of our example, we created a long document with one page for each letter to see the results of the mail merge.

By selecting Printer instead of New Document in the Merge to: drop-down list box, you can print the letters directly without needing to use this intermediate step.

Advanced mail merge techniques

THE FIRST step-by-step exercise demonstrates how a mail merge consists of two documents, the form letter and the data source. These combine together to create the finished document, which can then be printed out (or faxed or emailed). We've explained the essence of the form letter so now we're going to look in more detail at the data source to show how you can sort your records and customize your mailshot. For this example, we're going to create a new field, specifying whether or not parents are members of the school PTA council, and then create a mailing that goes only to those who are.

1 Open the data source document (saved opposite as Parents). You will see your database of names and addresses displayed as a Word table, with field names across the top and one row for each person.

2 Word has a special Database toolbar you can use with your mail merge data. Click on the View menu, then Toolbars and select the Database option.

3 When the toolbar appears, click on the Manage Fields button to bring up a dialog box that allows you to change the fields in the database.

4 You can now add extra fields: type a new field name into the box at the top left and press the Add button (we've added 'PTA council'). Click on the OK button.

5 You'll see the PTA council field appear as a new column in your table of information. Add the word 'Yes' to a couple of the rows in your names and addresses database. When you have made these changes, save the document.

6 Now open the Sports letter you created opposite. Click on the Mail Merge Helper button on the Mail Merge toolbar.

7 In the dialog box that pops up, click the Query Options button in the bottom section.

8 The Query Options dialog box has two tabs that allow for advanced mail merge options. Select the Filter Records tab and use the first drop-down list box to locate the PTA_council field.
   Note: Word needs to add the underscore character (_) between 'PTA' and 'council' in order to use it. You can ignore it for now.

9 Click on the Comparison box and select the Is not blank option from the list. Then click the OK button.

10 Now click the Merge button in the Mail Merge Helper. When the dialog box pops up, leave the default settings as they are and click Merge. As before, Word will create a new document containing all your letters – but this time you won't have a letter for those people for whom the PTA council field is blank.

CENTRALIZING YOUR DATA

As you start to use your computer for making small databases, such as the names and addresses in this example, you may find that the information overlaps with other databases – perhaps a basic address book that you use. The best idea is to put all the information into a central pool. The information can then be used for letters, invitations and newsletters – in fact, any mail merge document that you wish. This means that you don't have to type in the same details several times.

Working with percentages

Percentages are used in all sorts of calculations, from personal finance to a detailed business plan. So whether you are trying to sort out your tax or help with some maths homework, here's how Excel can help you to get the right answers.

Working out percentages is one of the most common mathematical operations after basic addition, multiplication, subtraction and division. That's why many calculators have a special percentage key. In a similar way, Excel makes it very easy to calculate a percentage.

On the next page, we'll work through some straightforward problems to see how to do this. In practice, it's probably quicker to use a calculator for such simple examples. But as with other tasks, the beauty of learning how to use Excel is that you can set up a detailed worksheet containing large numbers of figures that will be recalculated automatically every time the data changes. This is the basis of tables that can be used for calculating things, such as the profit on a small business venture, or even the odds on a series of bets.

Many common sums are expressed as percentages. Obvious examples are the VAT rate (currently 17.5%), interest rates (10% a year, perhaps), or a business profit margin (30%, say). All these factors can be included in a spreadsheet calculation and are easy to enter into Excel.

All you need to do is to use the % symbol together with the percentage factor and type this into the cell where it applies. Suppose you want to find the VAT on a purchase costing £63. This can be written out in the form of a simple calculation: £63 x 17.5%. To input this into Excel, you would write it out as =63*17.5%. If you type this into an empty cell in Excel, it will work out the result for you and display the answer: 11.025. Opposite, we show how to set up some percentage calculations in your worksheet.

Excel automates the calculation of percentages with a special percent button, so you will be able to plough through your work in no time at all.

CALCULATING PERCENTAGES

The word percentage comes from Latin and means 'out of a hundred'. It's used as a simple way of showing how any two numbers are related by referring them to the single standard number 100.

The advantage of this is that it makes it very easy to compare wildly different sums. For example, it can be hard to say whether 9/13 is bigger than 747/1189 without working them out, until you are told that one figure is roughly 69 percent and the other 62 percent. These figures are worked out by calculating the fraction (e.g. 9/13 is 1 ÷ 13 x 9 which equals 0.6923) and multiplying by 100 (to get 69.23%).

Any fraction can be expressed in this way. If it is less than 1, it will be expressed as a percentage less than 100 (so a half is 50%, three-quarters is 75%). If it is more than 1, it will be a percentage more than 100 (so 2 is 200% and 4½ is 450%).

Calculating percentage increases

One of the commonest uses for a percentage calculation is to add a factor to an existing sum and display the result. Here we show you how.

1 It's your lucky day! You have been given a pay rise of 8.5%, and you want to find out what difference this will make to your yearly salary. Start your worksheet by typing in some simple text labels in three consecutive cells (A1, B1 and C1) for Salary, Increase and New Salary. The cells underneath these headings will be used for our figures and calculations.

	A	B	C	D
1	Salary	Increase	New Salary	
2				
3				

2 Type your salary, say £18,000, into cell A2 and then move to the next cell across to type in the percentage increase of 8.5%.

	A	B	C
1	Salary	Increase	New Salary
2	18000	8.5%	

3 Move to the New Salary column and enter the formula that will calculate your new salary. Multiply the old salary by the percentage increase and add the answer to the old salary. Type the formula =A2*B2+A2. This works without brackets because Excel does the multiplication before the addition.

	A	B	C
1	Salary	Increase	New Salary
2	18000	8.50%	=A2*B2+A2

4 When you press the [Enter] key, Excel will calculate the correct answer. Now, if you change the number in cell B2 – perhaps you negotiated a better pay rise – the result will change automatically.

C
New Salary
19530

Calculating a percentage discount

1 You are considering setting up 10 special telephone numbers to save 5% off your bill. However, as the scheme costs £5.00 per quarter, you need to know whether this would be of benefit to you. Type in four column headers, and enter your quarterly bill and discount.

	A	B	C	D
1	Quarterly bill	Discount	Saving	Profit or loss?
2	180	5%		

2 Move to the Saving column and enter the formula to calculate the expected savings: =A2*B2. Press the [Enter] key to see the result.

C
Saving
9

B	C	D
Discount	Saving	Profit or loss
5%	=A2*B2	

3 Now move to the Profit or loss? column and enter a formula to see if you will save or lose money. Type in = C2-5, which is the saving less the £5 running costs. You will save £4. Now try changing the quarterly bill. If the answer is positive, this is how much you save each quarter. If it is negative, the scheme will cost you money.

D
Profit or loss?
4

	A	B	C	D
1	Quarterly bill	Discount	Saving	Profit or loss?
2	180	5%	9	=C2-5

HOW TO SUBTRACT A DISCOUNT

A common problem is to find out how much is left after applying a discount. One easy way to do so is to take the percentage discount away from 100, which shows the percentage remaining. For example, a 5% discount would leave 95%. Type =180*95% into a cell and check that the new bill is £171.

Excel at mini-databases

So far, we have used Excel for accounts and financial purposes, but Excel can handle text as well as numbers and will help you organize anything from a Christmas card address list to a gem collection.

Excel's worksheet is made up of rows and columns of cells. So far, we have mostly put numbers into these cells, but Excel is designed to organize text information as well as numbers. In fact, Excel can be used to create what is called a database, which is basically a list of items organized into different categories. There are other full-scale database programs, but Excel is capable of doing the work just as well for small-scale jobs.

For example, a database makes the perfect electronic address book. Opposite, we show you how to set up a database address book in Excel. You can use it for tasks such as making Christmas card or wedding invitation lists or any other occasion where you might need separate lists for separate events.

● On top form

Excel's database has many other useful functions. If you are involved with a club, for example, you'll find it a great way to store a membership list. Or, if you collect things such as stamps or minerals, you can use the Excel database to catalogue and label them.

What makes an Excel database so useful is that it makes lists easy to sift through, even when they have become long and involved. One way it does this is with a facility called Form view, which lets you see one record or entry at a time. To look at data in Form view,

first click on any record within your list. Next, select the Form option from the Data menu. You will see a new window pop up in the middle of your Excel screen. It also shows one record at a time, starting with the first one. Each field is shown in its own box. A set of buttons on the right-hand side allows you to flick backwards or forwards through your list, one record at a time. Other options let you add new ones and delete old ones. This way of viewing information is extremely efficient and easier to work with as you only have to concentrate on one record at a time.

Using an Excel database for an address book helps you get rid of all those scraps of paper on which you have jotted down new addresses, cab names and so on.

If you have a large book collection stored in an Excel database, Form view will show you the complete record you have made for each book – author, title, publisher and format.

With an address book, Form view will bring up the complete name and address, plus any other information you have put on the record.

Making an address book

A record of names and addresses is useful to have on your computer. Here we show you how to make one.

1 The first task is to choose the headings you want to use. We've started with first names, last names and addresses in the first four columns, adding other headings for telephone numbers or email addresses. You could even put headings for anniversaries such as birthdays, or people to go on your Christmas card list.

2 The next job is to enter all the names, addresses and other details. Here we've typed lots of names and addresses straight into the Excel worksheet. As you can see, the worksheet soon becomes a confusing way to look at lots of names and addresses.

3 Let's try switching to a more convenient way of viewing the names and addresses. First, highlight any one of the cells containing information by clicking over it. Now go to the Data menu and select the Form command.

4 This is what Form view looks like. Notice how it displays our list one record at a time, with each piece of data (or field) in its own text box. The buttons on the right let us step backwards and forwards through records, add new ones and delete old ones. To begin, click on Find Next.

5 Now we're looking at the second record in our address book. We can repeat the process by pressing the Find Next button until we reach the last record. We can also work backwards through the records. To go back to the first record, simply press the Find Prev button.

6 To add a new record to our address book, press the New button, type the new information into the text boxes and press the [Enter] key. You will see the new record appear in the worksheet and the Form view empty, ready for you to add another new record.

7 Now let's delete an old record we don't need any more. Use the Find Prev and Find Next buttons to locate the right record and press the Delete button.

8 As a safety precaution, Excel asks you if you're sure you want to delete the record. Press the OK button to confirm your decision and you will see that the record disappears from the Form and also from the table of information in the worksheet. To close the Form view and return to the worksheet, just click on the Close button. Save your changes as usual, using the Save command in the File menu.

Conditional formatting

We've already seen how you can apply formatting to make cells more noticeable. Excel can also be set up to apply formatting automatically to draw your attention to important developments.

Making cells stand out from the rest of a worksheet – by changing their text style and background colour, for example – is a handy feature of Excel. We know that Excel makes it easy to add such simple formatting (see Stage 1, pages 56-57), but wouldn't it be useful if you could use the formatting to make a cell stand out, depending on the value of the data in it? You can do this by hand, but it would be especially valuable to get Excel to do this automatically.

For example, let us imagine you use a worksheet to keep track of the payments in and out of your bank account. Wouldn't it be great if your bank-balance cell automatically turned red whenever you went into overdraft? Well, Excel can do this using a process known as conditional formatting.

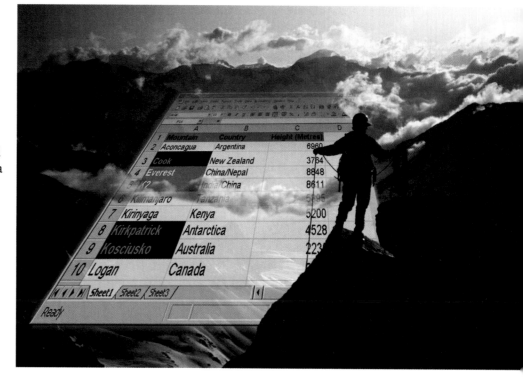

● Balancing the books

Conditional formatting is so called because it allows you to set a condition at which Excel will automatically format a cell. In the

	A	B	C	D	E	F
1	Item	Date	Payments	Receipts	Balance	
2	January Salary	02/01/01		£800.00		
3	Rent	03/01/01	£220.00			
4	Supermarket	06/01/01	£35.66			
5	Petrol	11/01/01	£15.02			
6	Supermarket	14/01/01	£31.45			
7						
8	Totals		£302.13	£800.00	£497.87	
9						
10						

	A	B	C	D	E	F
1	Item	Date	Payments	Receipts	Balance	
2	January Salary	02/01/01		£800.00		
3	Rent	03/01/01	£220.00			
4	Supermarket	06/01/01	£35.66			
5	Petrol	11/01/01	£15.02			
6	Supermarket	14/01/01	£31.45			
7	Holiday Booking	21/01/01	£500.00			
8						
9	Totals		£802.13	£800.00	-£2.13	
10						

To start with, our bank-balance in cell E8 is healthy and Excel displays it (top). However, as soon as we add our holiday booking payment, the bank account becomes overdrawn. Our attention is drawn to it by making Excel turn the cell red.

example (left), the conditional formatting applies only when your bank-balance cell reaches a condition of less than zero.

Every time a new entry is made on your worksheet, Excel automatically checks the bank-balance cell's value to see if the set condition has been reached. Of course, you don't have to set the condition at zero, you can choose any figure you wish and apply it to any cell. For example, you might get Excel to turn the bank-balance cell orange if it falls below £200, to warn you that you could be in danger of overdrawing.

You can use conditional formatting for many different types of worksheet. Supposing you are doing a research project on mountains and you have entered details of the heights of various peaks on your worksheet. Excel can be set up to highlight any mountains that exceed or fall short of your desired conditions. You could get Excel to show all the mountains that are over 7000m in one colour and those that are below 5000m in another.

WHAT IT MEANS

CONDITION

A condition allows Excel to make decisions based on a statement being true or false. It's usually combined with an action if the answer is true.

A longhand version of our formatting example looks like this: 'If the figure in cell E9 is less than zero, then change the cell colour to red'. The condition in this example is 'E9 is less than zero'. If it's true, the action occurs; if it is false, then nothing happens.

Applying conditional formatting

We are going to use the example of a worksheet containing a list of the tallest mountains in different countries to show how to apply conditional formatting.

PC TIPS

To locate which cells have conditional formats, choose Go To in the Edit menu and click Special in the dialog box. Click Conditional formats and then click OK.

1 Here is a worksheet listing mountains by their country and height. At a glance it is hard to tell from the worksheet which mountains are over 7000m or under 5000m. However, we can use conditional formatting to pick them out.

2 Let's start by trying to give the mountains rising to over 7000m a different background colour. Use the mouse to highlight all the cells that contain mountain heights and then go to the Format menu and select the Conditional Formatting option.

3 This will bring up the Conditional Formatting dialog box. You set conditions and actions by changing the text in each box and using the Format button.

4 The first box contains 'Cell Value Is', which is OK, so click on the down arrow at the right end of the second drop-down box and select greater than.

5 The dialog box changes to provide a window in which you enter your condition. Type 7000 into this box. Then click on the Format button.

6 Use the Font tab in the Format Cells dialog box (left) to change the text to yellow and the Patterns tab to change cell shading to red. Click on OK to close. To return to the worksheet, click on OK in the Conditional Formatting dialog box. Heights over 7000m show up as yellow on red (right).

7 While this gets the point across, we'd prefer to emphasize the names of the mountains rather than their heights. To do this, first remove the conditional formatting that you originally set up. Highlight the same cells as in Step 2, then bring up the Conditional Formatting dialog box and click on Delete. Excel asks you to confirm your choice. Select the Condition 1 checkbox, click on OK and return to the worksheet.

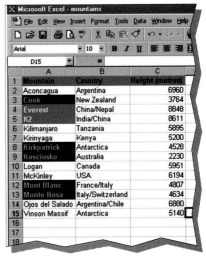

8 Now select the cells containing the mountain names (cells A2 to A15 in our example) and bring up the Conditional Formatting dialog box. Choose the Formula Is option in the first drop-down box and type =$C2>7000 in the new text box. Use the Format button to set the cell formatting as in Step 6.

10 You can now see how the worksheet reflects two sets of conditions. By using formulae in conditions, you'll find that you can give your worksheets more built-in intelligence.

9 Click the Add button and the dialog box expands to let you apply another condition. Use the Formula Is option, type in the formula =$C2<5000 and use the Format button to set a different format (left). Press the OK button.

Advanced cell formatting

Detailed entries on a worksheet can take up too much space if they are kept on a single line. Excel includes several tools that help you format text and keep your worksheet neat, tidy and readable.

S o far, you have seen how to apply simple formatting effects to worksheet cells in Excel and how to change the background colour of cells and the colour, size and font of text by using the Formatting toolbar (see Stage 1, pages 56-57). Now you'll see how you can add all sorts of text alignment options to your formatting skills to make your worksheets much easier to read and understand.

● **When the text won't fit**

These options are a great help when you have a few cells that contain very long lines of text. Normally this text overlaps into the cells next to them. If you want to constrain some text to fit the width of the cell it's in, you can get Excel to 'wrap' it. This converts it into a miniature paragraph (bottom left).

Excel even makes it a simple drag-and-drop affair to change the angle of text in a cell (as shown inset right). You can even specify an exact angle for the rotation. Alternatively, you can make text appear in a vertical stack, which is very useful if you need a narrow column.

Another advanced formatting option is Merge cells. By joining adjacent cells into one cell you can make your worksheet easier to use. For example, if you have a three-column table, you can combine the three cells above the table into a single cell for a heading using the alignment commands.

By using Excel's advanced – but simple – formatting options, you can rid yourself of many awkward text problems. You can make a long line of text wrap as a mini-paragraph (above left) and make a table heading sit in the centre of a range of cells (above right).

● **Formatting cells**

While you can carry out some of Excel's alignment options directly from the toolbar, the more powerful commands are only available through the Format Cells dialog box. This has an Alignment tab which includes all the alignment options.

You need only select the cells you want to format and bring up this dialog box to use the commands. After you follow the exercise on the next page, you will soon get the hang of even the most advanced options. Don't be afraid to experiment. Practise with a dummy worksheet if you are worried about your data.

WHAT IT MEANS

MERGE CELLS
Until now, all our Excel examples have used a regular grid of cells – with all cells in a column the same width and all cells in a row the same height. Excel also allows you to merge adjacent cells so one cell spans more than one column or row.

Formatting text in cells

You can use the Cells command from the Format menu to align text in cells and make your worksheets not only more attractive, but also easier to read. Here's an example of a worksheet containing text only. We'll improve its overall legibility by formatting.

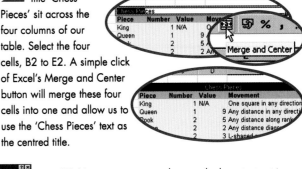

Microsoft® Excel

INDENTED LISTS

You may find that for some types of table a small indent helps readability. By using the Indent option you can specify the exact amount. First select the cells you want to indent, bring up the Alignment tab and increase the Indent setting. This is a tidy way to make lists with several sections easier to read – as shown in this example of fruit and vegetables.

1 Enter an easy table like this. We've used simple formatting to widen column E and add colour and emphasis.

2 We want to make our title 'Chess Pieces' sit across the four columns of our table. Select the four cells, B2 to E2. A simple click of Excel's Merge and Center button will merge these four cells into one and allow us to use the 'Chess Pieces' text as the centred title.

3 Highlight the four sub-headings from B3 to E3. Select Cells from the Format menu (or see PC Tips, below). Click on the Alignment tab in the Format Cells dialog box and use the mouse to rotate the Text pointer below Orientation to roughly 45 degrees. Click the OK button to see the result (inset).

4 Now we want to make sure the long text entries in the Movement column don't run outside our coloured columns. Highlight the cells (E4 to E9 in our example) and go to the Alignment options again. On the left of the dialog box you will see three Text control options: tick the Wrap text checkbox and press the OK button. You'll see the long text lines wrap into paragraphs within the cells.

5 However, where cells have become taller to allow the text to fit, text in the rest of the row stays at the bottom of the cells. This looks a little odd (right inset), but it can be altered. First, select all the cells in the table (B4 to E9 in this example).

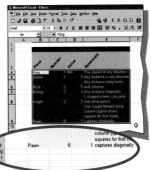

6 Bring up the Alignment tab again. Under the Text alignment section, you will see two drop-down boxes that control the position of text in cells. Click on the drop-down list box under the Vertical label. Select the Top option and press the OK button to apply this change.

PC TIPS

You can also bring up the Format Cells dialog box by using the right mouse button. Once you've got used to it, you'll find this is a lot quicker than using Excel's menu bar. First select the cells you want to format, then click once on the highlighted cells with the right mouse button. You will see a small pop-up menu; one of its options is the Format Cells command. Select this and you will see the usual dialog box.

7 For the final touch, we'll use a simpler alignment option to centre the text in the cells under the Number and Value sub-headings. First, highlight the cells (C4 to D9 in our table on the right), then press the Center button on Excel's formatting toolbar.

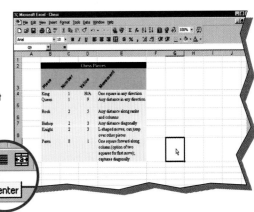

Understanding cell references

We have seen how Excel puts references into formulae so that it can make calculations. It's not essential to know exactly how this works but, as usual, an understanding of the basics helps avoid mistakes.

Performing calculations is incredibly easy when you use Excel. For example, if you want to add the contents of cells A1 and A2, with the result appearing in A3, just type =A1+A2 in cell A3. You can change the numbers in cells A1 and A2 and Excel still updates the result in cell A3.

The key to all this is the way Excel allows you to refer to cells by their row (as a number) and column (as a letter) co-ordinates. These cell references (A1, B3, X86, etc.) are a fundamental part of Excel, so it's well worth spending some time getting to grips with how cell references work if you want to get the most out of Excel.

In particular, Excel also uses these cell references to keep your calculations up-to-date when you move cells around.

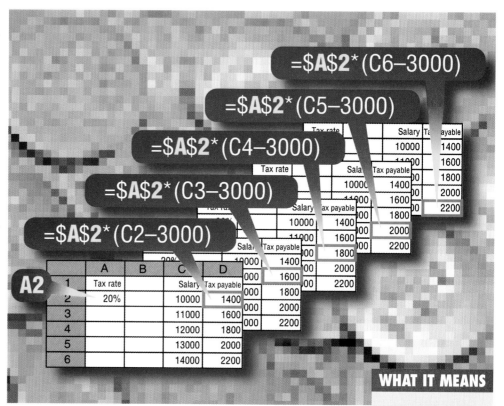

● Automatic updating

Type some numbers into cells A1 and A2 and the formula =A1+A2 into cell A3. Now insert a line before row 1 by clicking on cell A1 and selecting Rows from the Insert menu: you will see the numbers shift down one row.

The numbers and the sum are still the same, but surely the answer to the sum should be different as A1 and A2 have now both changed? Double click on cell A4, though, and you will see that Excel has changed your formula to =A2+A3.

Most of the time this automatic updating will prove extremely helpful because it saves time and effort. For example, if you have set up lots of calculations in your worksheet, you don't want to go through manually updating them all just because you have added a new row or column.

● Relative and absolute cell references

In our simple example, Excel changes the formula. This is because the references we originally typed (the 'A1' and 'A2' in =A1+A2) are relative cell references and can change according to the cell in which they appear. As another example, type some numbers into cells B2 and B3. Now copy the formula from cell A4 (select Copy from the Edit menu) and paste it into B4 (select Paste from the Edit menu). Excel guesses that you want to add the figures in the B column and changes the cell references in the calculation: the formula it puts in cell B4 is =B2+B3.

However, for some calculations, you won't want Excel to change the cell references. In order to do this you need to use an absolute cell reference instead of a relative one. We show you how to do this on the next page.

Using absolute cell references

Working through this exercise will pay off in the long run. Absolute cell references have many uses – especially for constant factors, such as the one set up here.

1 We'll start with the simple tax calculator. Type the information shown here into a blank worksheet. Unlike our previous worksheet (see Stage 2, pages 66-67), we've brought the tax rate out to a separate cell (B1) so we can take advantage of absolute cell referencing.

This basic layout now allows us to calculate the salary after tax for more than one member of the household, but requires the tax rate to be entered only once.

2 The first step is to add a formula to calculate Jane Green's salary after tax. This formula must work out the taxable salary after allowances, calculate the tax payable and deduct it from the salary to produce the salary after tax. It sounds complicated, but a single formula can do it.

In cell B6, type =B4-(B4-B5)*B1/ 100 and press the [Enter] key. Excel calculates the net salary.

PC TIPS

Cells in other worksheets

We have shown you how to set up workbooks that consist of several worksheets. Excel also lets you create formulae that refer to cells in other worksheets, by using an exclamation mark with the worksheet name and the cell. All you need to do is include the name of the worksheet as part of the cell reference. For example: to multiply the contents of cell A1 in Sheet1 by cell A2's contents in Sheet2 and have the result placed in a cell in Sheet3, you would type =Sheet1!A1 *Sheet2!A2 into any of Sheet3's cells.

3 Now let's see what happens when we copy this formula into cell C6 to calculate Mary Green's salary after tax. Click on cell B6, choose Copy from the Edit menu, move to cell C6 and then select Paste from the Edit menu to paste in the formula.

4 Excel has automatically updated the relative cell references in our formula, so the cells B1, B4 and B5 have been replaced with C1, C4 and C5. Unfortunately, in this case it has updated the B1 reference to C1, which is blank, so the calculation is wrong. We need to keep the reference to cell B1.

5 Let's replace the relative reference in the original formula. Click on cell B6, move to the formula bar and change B1 to $B$1. When you press the [Enter] key, you'll see the result is still the same.

=B4-(B4-B5)*$B$1/100

6 Copy the formula from cell B6 into cell C6. You'll notice that Excel now gets the calculation right.

= C4-(C4-C5)*$B$1/100

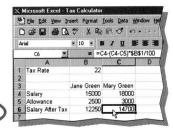

7 Now, let's imagine we want to add another row of information to this worksheet, such as details of another taxation rate. Right-click on the grey square at the left end of row 1 on the worksheet and choose Insert from the menu that appears. Then type in the information in cells A1 and B1.

8 Notice how the formulae in cells B7 and C7 still calculate the correct result. This is because Excel can automatically update absolute cell references as well as relative cell references when you modify a worksheet. Click on cell C7 and look at the formula that's displayed in the Formula Bar. You can see that the absolute references to cell B1 have been updated to those for cell B2.

Microsoft® Excel

Hiding rows and columns

What do you do when you don't want to be distracted from important parts of your worksheet by masses of other information? The simple answer is to hide the sections that you don't need.

As you become more experienced with Excel, you're likely to start constructing more complex worksheets containing larger tables of information. Sometimes this will make it difficult to pick out important facts and figures – such as annual or monthly totals – from a mass of unwanted detail.

As we've already seen, we can use cell formatting to make important cells stand out in another colour or font (see pages 58-59). But what do you do if you want to see the really important figures on-screen without having to scroll backwards and forwards through a large worksheet?

● Concealing information

The solution is to conceal all the detailed information when you aren't using it. Excel lets you do this by hiding complete rows and columns of a worksheet. Don't worry about accessing the data. When you hide a row or column, all the figures and formulae contained within its cells are remembered and used by Excel. And it is just as simple to unhide this information as it is to hide it.

All you have to do to hide a row of figures on a worksheet is to select it, click on the Format menu, click on the Row option and select Hide from the sub-menu that appears. You can use the same technique to hide a column, too.

Of course, Excel also makes it possible for you to retrieve any rows or columns that you

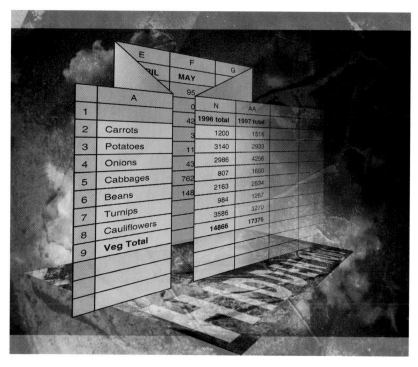

Show only the main rows or columns in your document by hiding unnecessary text.

have hidden. You might be wondering how it's possible to do this if you can't see a hidden row to select it. The answer is easy: you just highlight the two rows on either side of the hidden one. Then go to the Format menu, position the mouse pointer on the Row option and choose Unhide from the sub-menu that appears.

Here's a typical table of information (left) relating to a family greengrocery business. The monthly sales totals contain lots of detailed figures for individual items, but it's quite hard to see the 'big picture'. By hiding the rows of individual fruit and vegetable figures (below) it's a lot easier to see how overall fruit and vegetable sales vary from one month to the next.

Microsoft Excel - Brown's Grocers

File Edit View Insert Format Tools Data Window Help

Arial   10   B I U

A1

	A	B	C	D	E	F	G
1		Jan	Feb	Mar	Apr	May	Jun
2	Carrots	34	96	22	5	6	11
3	Potatoes	656	56	43	44	95	324
4	Onions	88	34	65	21	0	65
5	Cabbages	78	23	68	11	42	24
6	Beans	23	667	432	43	3	77
7	Turnips	675	35	57	762	11	33
8	Cauliflowers	345	657	9	148	612	668
9	Veg Total	1899	1568	696	1034	769	1202
10	Apples	55	0	67	1	11	88
11	Pears	3	67	53	62	565	45

Microsoft Excel - Brown's Grocers

File Edit View Insert Format Tools Data Window Help

Arial   10   B I U $ % ,

A1

	A	B	C	D	E	F	G	H	I
1		Jan	Feb	Mar	Apr	May	Jun	Jul	Aug	Sep
9	Veg Total	1899	1568	696	1034	769	1202	1618	1705	319
19	Fruit Total	582	1198	625	285	813	685	672	2876	37
20										
21										

WHAT IT MEANS

UNHIDE
The Unhide option is the reverse of the Hide option and is used to make hidden rows or columns visible again. If you want to reveal all the hidden rows and columns in a worksheet at once, click on the grey button in the top left corner of the worksheet before choosing the Unhide option.

	E2
	A
1	
2	Carrots
3	Potatoes
4	Onions
	Cabb

How to conceal unwanted data

With continued use, a worksheet can grow in size. Hiding the greater part of the information it contains can make it easier to see the overall picture.

1 To illustrate how hiding rows and columns works, we've set up a table of sales figures for a family greengrocery business, but you can use any worksheet for the following steps. In our worksheet, we want to make it easier to see how the overall monthly fruit and vegetable sales compare.

2 Let's hide the row of figures for carrots. Select the Carrots row by clicking on the grey button at the left end of the row. Click on the Format menu and then select Hide from the Row options. You'll see that Row 2 disappears from view, but the row below is unaltered.

3 Even though Row 2 can't be seen, its data is still present and calculations that include the carrot sales figures are still correct. For example, the totals in the Veg Total row stay the same.

8	**Cauliflowers**	345
9	**Veg Total**	1899
10	**Apples**	55

4 Hide the other rows of individual vegetables by selecting them all at once and using the same menu selection as in Step 2.

5 Here's how to restore the hidden rows whenever you want to look at, or update, any of the detailed figures. Use the mouse to highlight the first two rows of the worksheet, where Rows 2 to 8 are hidden. Then go to the Format menu and select Unhide from the Row options.

PC TIPS

A Quicker Way to Hide

There's a quicker way to hide rows and columns than going through the Format menu and sub-menus. Once you've selected your rows or columns by clicking on the grey buttons, simply click the right mouse button and then choose the Hide option from the menu. Unhide works in the same way.

6 You can also hide a column of a worksheet. Let's use this to pick out the February sales figures. Highlight the January column, go to the Format menu and position the mouse pointer on the Column option. Then select Hide from the sub-menu that appears.

7 As with the rows, it's also possible to hide more than one column at a time. Use the mouse to select all the other columns of monthly figures after February. Go to the Format menu and choose Hide from the Column sub-menu.

8 You can restore hidden columns when you want to see the other monthly figures again. Start by highlighting the first three columns of the worksheet with the mouse. Go to the Format menu, position the mouse pointer over the Column option and choose Unhide from the sub-menu.

9 Of course, you can combine hiding columns with hiding rows at the same time. We've used the options on the Row and Column sub-menus of the Format menu so that only the annual totals for the fruit and veg tables are visible.

Make charts look great

Do you want to give your charts and graphs a more professional image?
Here are the secrets of how to make great-looking charts with Excel.

We have already seen how to use Excel to create graphs and charts from the data stored in your worksheets (see Stage 1, pages 58-59). But, with a little extra effort, you can make your graphs and charts really leap off the page.

Once Excel has created a chart, customizing it is as simple as clicking on the part you want to change with the right mouse button. For example, you can choose to work on the chart's title, its legend (or key) or the data points that make up the actual chart.

You can format a chart element in much the same way as you would a worksheet cell. This means you can apply font, alignment and background-pattern formats to the chart's title, add special effects to the bars or pie segments in your charts, and much more. As you experiment with the techniques shown opposite, you'll find that different options for varying chart elements are available, depending on whether you're editing a pie chart, bar chart or line graph.

● Quick results

You can select individual elements by clicking on them in the chart itself. A right click will bring up a menu of the formatting tools. For example, if you're working on a segment of a pie chart, you can apply a wide range of colours, patterns and fills. As an even more impressive fill, you can use any photograph or drawing that you have stored as a graphics file. Opposite, we show how to enhance a pie chart comparing school sports by using pictures of the activities themselves.

WHAT IT MEANS

DATA POINTS

A data point is the element of a chart that represents a particular value in your worksheet. For example, in a pie chart each segment is a data point. In a bar chart each bar of the graph is a data point. In a line graph each point plotted on the line is a data point.

We know how to make individual elements of graphs and charts colourful, but with a little extra knowledge, customized colours and pictures can also be incorporated.

Making more attractive pie charts

You can use some of Excel's advanced charting tools to give a simple pie chart a unique and much more impressive look. Below we show you how.

FOR THIS example, we have entered some data and created a pie chart using Excel's Chart Wizard. We followed the basic method covered in Stage 1, pages 58-59, in order to set up an imaginary chart of a school class's favourite sports.

1 Use the mouse to select the segment of the pie chart that represents football.

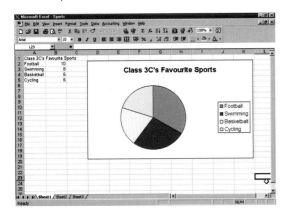

2 Right-click on the segment and then choose Format Data Point from the menu that appears.

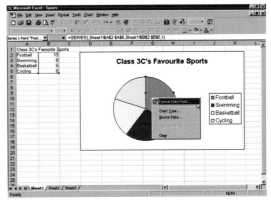

3 In the Format Data Point dialog box, make sure the Patterns tab is selected, then press the Fill Effects button.

PC TIPS

We've used the right mouse button to jazz up the sections of the pie chart here, but you can also use it to customize many other elements in the chart. The text can be formatted just like text in any worksheet cell. For example, right-click on the chart title.

You will see a pop-up menu with a Format Chart Title option. If you select this, you'll see a dialog box that lets you change the typeface, colour and alignment. Try experimenting with other chart objects.

4 The Fill Effects window gives us an impressive choice of ways to fill this slice of the pie chart with colour gradients, patterns and textures. However, we're going to use an image of a footballer – so go for the Picture tab and click on Select Picture.

5 Use the Select Picture dialog box to find the picture you want. We have selected this clip-art image from the CorelDRAW CD-ROM.

6 Click the OK button in the Fill Effects window and then the OK button. The football segment of the pie chart should now look like this.

7 Now repeat the process for the remaining three segments to fill them with appropriate pictures. The final result should look as professional as this.

The smart way to fill cells

Creating a useful worksheet can be quite arduous. However, Excel can lend a hand and save time – even when copying and pasting cells isn't appropriate.

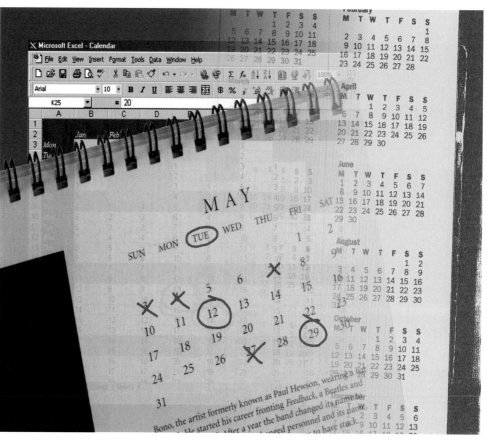

Excel provides you with more than one way of filling cells with the same type of data. For example, rather than having to copy and paste the same information repeatedly, Excel allows you to highlight specific cells, which can then be filled from the Edit menu. For adjacent cells, you can even drag the contents of one cell and drop them into another (see Stage 1, pages 54-55).

However, so far we have only used this feature to fill in cells using identical data. Now we are going to discover how to fill a range of cells automatically with, for example, ascending or descending numbers.

● Smart fills

You could fill cells A1 to A5 on a worksheet with the ascending numbers 100, 200, 300, 400 and 500. Excel also provides ways for you to fill cells with successive days, months or years. Most of these automated fills can be accomplished with a simple drag of the mouse. These so-called 'smart fills' are controlled from the Series option on the Fill sub-menu. If you select this, it opens a dialog box that offers you a choice of four fill types: Linear, Growth, Date and AutoFill.

● The four options

The Linear option is used to increase (or decrease) the values between cells by a fixed amount each time.

Growth works in a similar way, but by increasing the values between each cell exponentially – 1, 2, 4, 8, 16 and so on, for example. Date, obviously, refers to date-related data fills, allowing you to choose from day, month and year.

The fourth and final option, AutoFill, will assess the data already keyed into the first few highlighted cells and then automatically decide on which type of fill is necessary for the remaining cells.

Producing labour-intensive documents that incorporate long lists of headings can be made easy with Excel's AutoFill option. This makes preparing a complex workbook, based around a calendar perhaps, far less time-consuming.

PC TIPS

Excel will also let you add your own customized fill options. For example, you can set up a series of atomic elements to help with a science project. To do this, choose Options from the Tools menu and select the Custom Lists tab from the dialog box. Then, all you have to do is type in your list of elements and click on the Add button.

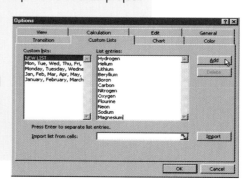

Saving time with smart fills

Here, as an example of how useful smart fills can be, we show you how quickly you can make a calendar for the whole year.

1 Start by consulting a calendar, then type in a few days and dates in January. As you can imagine, it would take ages to finish the calendar if we had to type in everything manually. Instead, we'll use Excel's smart fill tool.

2 First, we will fill in the month names. Highlight the cell containing Jan (cell B2 in our example) and the eleven cells to its right. Now select Fill from the Edit menu and choose Series from the sub-menu. Choose AutoFill from the Type section of the window and click on OK.

PC TIPS

There is a special mouse technique to help you use smart fills more efficiently.

Start with two adjacent cells in your series, say January in cell A1 and February in cell A2. Now highlight these two cells and drag the small black square downward.

As you do, Excel spots that January and February are part of a series and a small yellow tip pops up to show you successive months. Release the mouse button and Excel will fill the cells. This works for numbers and the days of the week.

3 The names of the months have appeared in the highlighted cells. Next, we'll add the remaining weekdays of the month. Highlight the cell containing Sun (in our example, cell A9) and the 31 cells below it. Again, select Fill from the Edit menu and choose Series from the sub-menu. As before, choose AutoFill and then click on OK.

4 The next job is to fill in the dates for January. Highlight the 31 cells that will contain the dates and bring up the Series dialog box again. Excel looks at the numbers that were already entered (Step 1) and suggests a linear series with a Step value of one between cells. Press the OK button.

5 Scroll to the bottom of the January dates. You can see that the 31st falls on a Wednesday. Scroll back up the worksheet and find the first Thursday in the February column. Type the number 1 and repeat Step 4, selecting this cell and the 28 cells below it.

6 Repeat Step 5 for the remaining months of the year, remembering to change the number of cells you highlight to reflect the number of days in each month.

7 Now, apply some cell and text formatting to add the finishing touches to your calendar and make it easier to read. Grey out the weekends and bank holidays and add a coloured fill to indicate the unused days at the top of the calendar.

Modifying text styles

With CorelDRAW, you aren't stuck with the basic typefaces that come with Windows. You can create new letters with striking, original shapes – even ones that look as if they are hewn from solid granite.

If you normally work with text using a program such as Word, you might think of type as pretty much a fixed element. Once you have chosen a font, you can change its size, style or colour, but not the basic shape of the characters.

With CorelDRAW, on the other hand, this is anything but the case. Type can be edited like any other object you create. In fact, CorelDRAW goes out of its way to provide tools to help with everything from basics, such as changing the colour and texture of text, to sophisticated options, such as creating your own customized typefaces.

● A choice of text styles

CorelDRAW is able to do this because of the way it handles vector-based images. It still uses ordinary fonts – exactly the same ones as you find in Word – but it allows you to convert them into shapes so that they behave like any other object drawn on the worksheet. From there, you can do with them what you will.

There are two types of text available in CorelDRAW: Paragraph Text and Artistic Text. Paragraph Text works in exactly the same way

as in Word: in fact, the text Property Bar looks very similar to the Formatting toolbar in Microsoft Word. It has all the same functions, allowing you to choose the font, alter the size, and add basic formatting commands such as Bold, Italic and Underline. And, of course, you can choose to align your text to the left, centre or middle, or to justify it. To make things easier, CorelDRAW uses the same icon symbols as Word for all these functions.

Artistic Text is most useful when you want to start playing around with text, by doing such things as adding special effects or altering its shape. It is the tool of choice for anyone who wants to create interesting logos, or who would like to produce more imaginative or decorative text effects.

WHAT IT MEANS

ARTISTIC TEXT
This is CorelDRAW's term for text to which you can apply special effects – distortion, extrusion, blending and so on (see Stage 2, pages 84-87). Artistic Text is created from the Text Tool.

● Creating imaginative effects

When text is first typed in using CorelDRAW's Text Tool, it is a fixed shape which can only be changed in basic ways, such as shrinking, moving and rotating it. However, you can convert the text into curved objects very easily. This adds object nodes to each character, which enables you to change its shape and edit it as if it were an ordinary CorelDRAW object.

Once text has been changed into curved objects, you can start applying a number of special effects to the text. Essentially, these are the same as the effects that can be used with any ordinary object, such as distortion, adding a texture or other pictorial effect and merging with other objects. However, by bringing a little imagination to the special effects you choose, and the way that you apply them, you can create some exciting images.

● First steps with Artistic Text

In the examples shown on the next page, we use the Envelope special effect to distort the text into dramatic shapes, using pre-set envelope designs and your own creations. We also look at how the use of colour effects can suddenly make text appear much more interesting and dynamic, either by using the

CREATING YOUR OWN TYPEFACE

Perhaps the most impressive thing you can do with text in CorelDRAW is to create your own typefaces. This is quite an involved process, but allows you the ultimate freedom when using text.

Instead of changing letters every time you want them to look different, you can define a set of characters for your own alphabet. This can then be saved and selected and used at any time in the future.

Of course, this will take some time, so if you don't fancy creating your own complete typeface from scratch, you can simply alter an existing one, which allows you to edit or replace only the existing letter shapes that you need.

Fountain fills from previous exercises or the amazing clip-art-like fills that come with CorelDRAW.

Finally, if you're really adventurous, you can start experimenting with the shapes of the letters. You've already learnt how to move and use nodes, and this works in exactly the same way.

Some advanced effects

CorelDRAW offers enormous scope for experimenting with Artistic Text. Here we show some of the most popular effects you can achieve in addition to the main examples that are shown in the step-by-step exercises.

As well as the examples on the following pages, you can produce many other effects. These include making text run round a shape or outline, as is often seen on badges and labels. Fitting text to a fixed path or outline (top) is easy, as you simply draw a curved line for the bottom of the letters to follow.

Bevelled text (middle), which looks as though it has been carved out of a solid material, is also easy to create using the built-in Bevelled tool and just a little bit of tweaking to ensure the text stays readable.

Realistic shadows can also be created from a copy of your original shape, which is then distorted and blurred to look as if the letters are solid and the shadow is being cast by a real light source (bottom).

Even features such as large, dropped capitals at the start of paragraphs, or text specially fitted inside irregularly shaped objects are relatively easy. The only real limit is your imagination, as you learn to use CorelDRAW's tools to create an infinite variety of effects.

Using Envelopes and Fills

A number of CorelDRAW's basic graphic effects work particularly well with text, and provide interesting results. Here we take a look at Envelopes and Fills.

1 Select the Text Tool from the toolbox. Click once with the mouse in the drawing area. A vertical bar will appear, which shows you where your text will begin to appear.

2 Before typing anything, use the Property Bar options. We'll start with a bold typeface. Click on the drop-down font list and scroll down to select Arial Black. You can also use the size drop-down box to choose a bigger size (24 point).

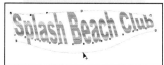
3 Now type your text. For the time being, keep the line of text quite short, as we have done here.

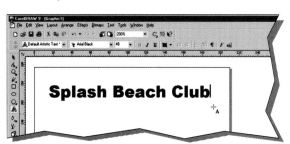

4 Select the text box and then click on the Interactive Envelope Tool which appears when you click on the small black arrowhead on the fourth tool from the bottom of the toolbox.

5 The Envelope toolbar appears. It includes several ready-made shapes for you to use. Click the Add Preset button and a drop-down list of shapes appears. Select one by clicking on it. You'll now see the text change to reflect the shape you chose.

6 We'll now use some colour effects to add more interest. Select the text box again and choose Favorite Fills and Outlines from the Scrapbook sub-menu of the Tools menu.

7 A folder containing small icons that represent the different texture patterns available appears. Double-click on one of them.

8 You will instantly see your line of text fill with the pattern you selected. If you want a different pattern, use the Fill Tool's Pattern Fill option to locate and select your bitmap pattern.

Changing the shapes of letters

We've given these letters a special twist to suit a Halloween party, but you can easily choose an example that will be more useful to you – perhaps using Artistic Text to create a personal logo.

1 Select the Text Tool from the toolbox. Once again we have chosen Arial Black and set it to 24 point (see Step 2 on the previous page). Click the cursor into the middle of the screen and type in your text.

2 In order to edit the letters with the Shape Tool you must first convert them to curves. Select the text with the Pick Tool and press the Convert To Curves button on the Property Bar.

3 At first, the text will look the same as before, but click on the Shape Tool and you'll see a large number of nodes appear around the two words.

PC TIPS

As you edit the nodes of a character, remember that it is now just like any other CorelDRAW shape. This means you can add and delete nodes as necessary.

To add a node, click on the outline with the Shape tool where you want the node to appear and then use the large plus button that appears at the far left of the Property Bar whenever you have the Shape Tool selected. The minus button can be used to remove a selected node.

4 Try altering the shape of some of the letters. Use the Shape Tool as normal to move the nodes (inset). You'll probably have to zoom in using the Zoom Levels drop-down menu on the toolbar to see them clearly. If you need an extra node, see PC Tips.

5 Remember that if things go wrong you can use the Undo button to go back and erase one action at a time. CorelDRAW, unlike Microsoft Paint, remembers all the actions you do, so you can undo your edits all the way back to the initial blank page. You can also reinstate them if you use Redo.

6 Now that the text has been converted to curves, you can use any ordinary object tool on the text in the same way as the Shape Tool. For example, you can change its colour. Try using a simple fill or, as we have done here, apply a Fountain fill (see Stage 2, page 83) to create the result shown below.

Introducing Corel PHOTO-PAINT

When you buy the CorelDRAW package, you also get lots of handy graphics extras. One of the most useful of them is PHOTO-PAINT.

PHOTO-PAINT is one of the two main programs supplied in the CorelDRAW package. However, unlike CorelDRAW, which is vector-based, PHOTO-PAINT is a bitmap-based paint package. This means that you work with pictures made up of thousands of dots, much as you do in Microsoft Paint (see Stage 1, pages 62-63). However, PHOTO-PAINT is far more advanced than Microsoft Paint and offers a much bigger range of features for creating and editing bitmap pictures.

Menu Bar
Nearly all Windows programs share the same basic features, of which the menu bar is one of the most important. PHOTO-PAINT is no exception, although its bar does contain a number of special options.

Standard Toolbar
This contains buttons for various common commands, such as File Open and File Save.

Property Bar
The basic layout of PHOTO-PAINT is very similar to that of CorelDRAW; in both programs the Property Bar changes according to which option or tool has been selected. The default setting shows information relating to the pick tool.

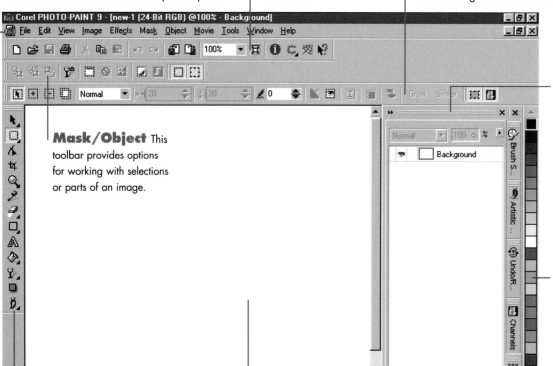

Mask/Object This toolbar provides options for working with selections or parts of an image.

Docker
PHOTO-PAINT uses a docker window, which can be hidden, to provide access to many different options. You can hide or show parts of images, tweak the paint brush settings and undo or redo past actions with this docker.

Palette
The palette is extremely versatile, and although it displays only a small number of colours by default, you can pick any colour that the human eye can distinguish, via one of four types of colour picker.

Toolbox
PHOTO-PAINT's toolbox is in a similar position to the one in CorelDRAW, but the tools available here are very different. Most are not object-based, and there is a wide variety of brushes and editing tools.

Canvas
This is where all the actual work and drawing is done. The default canvas size is quite small, but you can change it to any size you choose and to any colour or pattern.

Colours Used
This series of displays indicates the particular colour of paint you are using, the page you are painting on and the fill, if you choose to use it.

WHAT IT MEANS

OPACITY

The term 'opacity' refers to the degree to which an object or paint is transparent. Paint that is 100% opaque completely covers the background. Paint that is just 5% opaque is almost transparent.

● Advantages

If you've followed the Microsoft Paint exercises, you'll have realized that while it's adequate for simple pictures, even the most accomplished computer artist can create only rather basic and cartoon-like pictures with it. This is because it lacks any advanced tools and relies almost entirely on a few brush strokes, plus the steadiness of the user's hand.

PHOTO-PAINT, however, is much easier to use as it provides a greater degree of accuracy and has many additional features, such as safety nets, colourful fills, more realistic brush strokes and opacity. These tools help you to add more subtlety to your pictures than Microsoft Paint allows. For example, you can use softer, merging shading on a background, rather than having abrupt changes of colour. You can also soften the edges of an object.

● Realistic pictures

PHOTO-PAINT comes into its own when you are working with photographic images from a scanner or digital camera. The program enables you to adjust or edit the images in several different and important ways; for example, you can adjust the brightness and contrast to help make the picture clearer.

Get started with PHOTO-PAINT

How to start up PHOTO-PAINT and set up a blank window in which to work.

1 You will find the Corel PHOTO-PAINT program in the CorelDRAW folder.

2 When you start PHOTO-PAINT, you will see a welcome screen very similar to that used in CorelDRAW (see Stage 2, pages 68-69). You have six icons to choose from. For this exercise, click on the one at the top left, which is called New Image.

3 You will see a large dialog box with several sections. The options here control the following:

Color mode: This lets you choose how many colours your image should be displayed in. Usually, 24-bit RGB gives the best display quality.

Paper color: PHOTO-PAINT lets you choose any colour you like.

Image size: Think of this as 'paper size'. You can pick almost any size you wish.

Resolution: This lets you select how many pixels (dots) will be used for each inch (or centimetre) of your painting. The more dots that are used, the finer the detail in the image will be. The final parts include options for very advanced users.

4 For our first exercise we want to choose the exact number of pixels to use in our picture. Click on the box in Image size that currently says 'inches' (yours will have 'centimeters' if your PC is set up to work in metric units), and select pixels from the drop-down list.

5 Still in Image size, change the numbers used for the width and height to 400 and 300 and then press the OK button.

6 You will now see your blank image ready to use (right). PHOTO-PAINT shows your image in its own window inside the main PHOTO-PAINT window. This allows you to work on several pictures at once (unlike Microsoft Paint).

PHOTO-PAINT basics

Start by getting used to the main tools available in PHOTO-PAINT. Other tools can be added later as you become more familiar with the program.

IF THE HUGE number and variety of tools used in PHOTO-PAINT looks intimidating after the simple appearance of Microsoft Paint, it's worth trying some basic tools to see how they work. If you look down the toolbox you will see that some, such as the Rectangle Tool and Eraser, look the same as those in Paint. However, after a few minutes of experimentation, you'll soon see that these tools are much more powerful than Paint's.

1 We'll start by drawing a simple coloured shape on our blank image. First, select the Rectangle Tool from the toolbox on the left.

2 Now click with the right mouse button on a square in the colour palette on the right side of the screen. You will see the Fill box at the bottom of the screen change to indicate the colour you have chosen.

3 Draw a rectangle using the same click and drag technique you have used in Microsoft Paint and CorelDRAW (see Stage 1, page 63 and Stage 2, page 71). When you release the mouse button, PHOTO-PAINT immediately draws and fills in the rectangle.

4 Now try the Eraser Tool. Click once on the tool in the toolbox and then drag it through the blue rectangle. As you do so, you'll see that the path it has cleared through the blue rectangle has soft edges. This contrasts with Microsoft Paint's eraser, which leaves hard edges when it erases.

5 Now let's save this example. PHOTO-PAINT saves files in the same way as other Windows programs, so select Save As from the File menu (right).

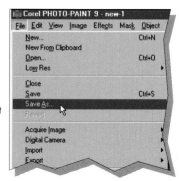

6 Use the Save in drop-down box to find your PC's My Files folder, then type in a name for this picture and press the Save button.

Note: PHOTO-PAINT uses its own file format (with the CPT extension), but it can also export pictures in many different formats for use in other programs (see PC Tips, right).

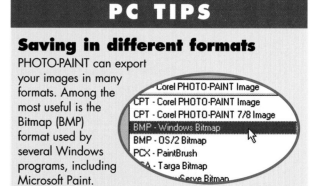

PC TIPS

Saving in different formats

PHOTO-PAINT can export your images in many formats. Among the most useful is the Bitmap (BMP) format used by several Windows programs, including Microsoft Paint.

PHOTO-PAINT's advanced tools

Extend your graphics capabilities using PHOTO-PAINT's advanced tools.

PHOTO-PAINT has many more advanced tools and options than the Microsoft Paint program. Although the tools are more sophisticated, they are easy to use once you have experimented a little. To give you some idea of how these tools can help you to create better pictures, we'll introduce you to some of the most commonly used ones below.

CorelDRAW™

Brush Types

PHOTO-PAINT has a huge number of brush types and styles – far more than Paint. You can specify just about every aspect of the brush, including its type (air brush, paint brush, and many more). You can also choose from several options that change the way 'paint' goes on to your 'canvas', such as its thickness.

Image Sprayer

This amazing tool paints with images; as you drag the pointer over your blank page, it leaves a trail of mini-pictures. PHOTO-PAINT has several ready-made image brushes: for this picture we've simply drawn an X on a blank screen using the foliage image brush. You can also create your own image brushes.

Fills

PHOTO-PAINT also provides you with many different fill options, just like CorelDRAW. Whereas Microsoft Paint has just one solid fill, PHOTO-PAINT also has fountain fills, texture fills and bitmap fills.

Smearing, smudging and blending

PHOTO-PAINT has other tools to edit your pictures, once you begin drawing them. The tools are able to smear, smudge or blend parts of your drawings. This helps to give them a more realistic and non-computerized look. You can also use these tools to customize the images stored on the CorelDRAW CD-ROMs for use in your own pictures.

Safety Nets

Where Microsoft Paint can undo only the last three commands, PHOTO-PAINT has a system of 'Safety Nets', which allow you to undo any number of commands. It presents the commands that you have carried out as a list, allowing you to see exactly what has happened in your painting.

Objects

PHOTO-PAINT can also use some of CorelDRAW's object-based drawing capabilities. Objects can be made to 'float' behind or in front of the bitmap image you are painting. You can also make objects transparent to create composite pictures.

Masks

You can create and edit masks for your pictures. These masks allow you to mark off parts of your picture to protect them from paint – just like masking tape does when you are painting a window frame. The difference is that PHOTO-PAINT masks can be absolutely any shape you like.

Editing Movies

You can even use PHOTO-PAINT to create and edit video movie files that you can play on your computer. You can use any of PHOTO-PAINT's tools on individual frames of a movie and then reassemble them into a complete film of your own making.

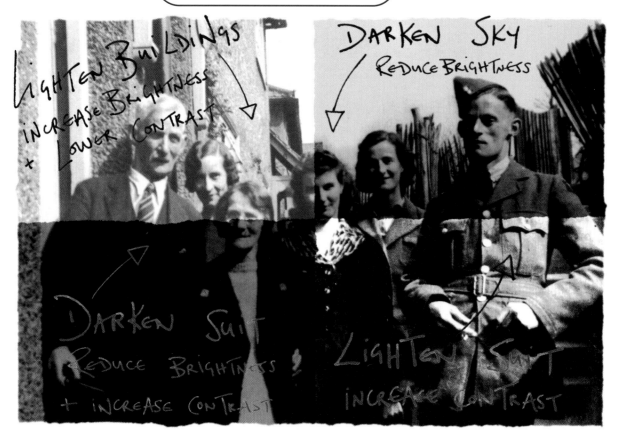

As well as having lots of fun with PHOTO-PAINT effects, you can also bring old photos – and the memories that they inspire – back to life.

Simple photo editing

Whether you have access to a scanner or not, the ability to alter photographs and other images is extremely useful – and exceedingly easy in Corel PHOTO-PAINT.

We have already seen how photographs and images can be reproduced on letters and documents (see Stage 1, pages 44-47), converted into background wallpaper for the Windows Desktop (see Stage 1, pages 68-69) or used in other paint packages.

But, with the right software, you can do so much more with your images. Once a photo has been scanned and saved on your computer (see page 107), you can use a program such as Corel PHOTO-PAINT to retouch it, to change the brightness and colour, to cut out parts of the picture or to add 2D and 3D effects.

● A change for the better
There are usually two reasons for making such changes. First, for example, you might want to improve the quality of your photograph before you use it again by enriching the colour and light. Alternatively, you might want to add some fun effects to

alter the picture – from something as simple (and fun) as changing the colour of your pet dog, to cutting out and pasting the heads of relatives onto other bodies!

● For greater effect
There is a wide range of effects available and all work in a similar, easy-to-understand way. Often, all you have to do is select the effect and apply it to your picture. You can even undo the effect if you don't like it and want to start again. Once you've learnt how to brighten an image, it's very easy to learn how to sharpen or blur it. If the original quality of the photo that was scanned is poor, you can even compensate for that as well by revitalizing faded areas or removing scratch marks and blemishes.

Whatever the task, serious or fun, PHOTO-PAINT should be able to help – and without a camera or darkroom in sight. We show you how to make a start on the opposite page.

WHAT IT MEANS

RETOUCH
This term refers to any alteration made to a completed picture, usually a scanned photograph. Retouching can be a minor process, such as making the picture slightly brighter, or a more substantial change, such as cutting out part of the picture and replacing it with a new image.

Retouching photographs

Here we show you how easy it is to make a number of amendments to a photograph – from simple contrast changes to more complex two-dimensional special effects.

CorelDRAW™

1 The photo we are going to retouch is a picture of a macaw. As you can see, the scan hasn't been done very well and the image is a bit too dark.

2 To change the brightness and contrast, click on the Image menu. Choose the Adjust option and select the Brightness-Contrast-Intensity option.

PC TIPS

You don't need a scanner if you want to practise retouching photos. There are plenty of photo images on the CorelDRAW CD-ROMs for you to use, or you can import a photo image from someone else's PC or the Internet.

You will find plenty of photo images on disk three of the CorelDRAW CD-ROMs. Use PHOTO-PAINT's Open command to retrieve the photos directly from the CD-ROM.

3 A new window appears, containing several controls. The Brightness, Contrast and Intensity slider bars work much like the controls of a television set or PC monitor. To change the brightness, move the slider bar to the left for a darker image or to the right for lighter one. If the Preview button (inset) is pressed, you can see the effect of your changes to the image.

4 You can change the Contrast and Intensity in the same way. Experiment and check your changes with the Preview button. If your changes make the picture worse, simply press the Cancel button or move the sliders to a new position and preview the result. Click the OK button when you're happy with your changes.

5 If you want to try something more exciting, there are lots of special effects you can apply to the picture. We'll try one of the Distort effects, called Pixelate. This will stylize your picture so that it is composed of much larger blocks of colour. From the Effects menu, select the Distorts option and choose the Pixelate option.

6 The Pixelate dialog box works similarly to the Brightness-Contrast-Intensity box. You can change the shape of the pixels with Pixelate mode. We've selected Radial, so the colour blocks seem to revolve around the centre of the picture. Use the sliders in the Adjust section to alter their width and height. The smaller the pixels are, the clearer the picture will be. We've chosen 5 to give a blurred effect. Use the Opacity slider to set how much the original picture shows through. When finished, click OK.

7 You'll now see the difference you can make to any image with just a few mouse clicks. Try some of the other options under the Effects menu to see what other changes you can make. As always, don't be afraid to experiment.

Resizing pictures

You might have found exactly the right picture that you were looking for, but if it is five times larger than your screen or printer paper, you're going to have to learn how to shrink it to fit.

Any computerized picture has its own specific shape and size, which can be measured using a number of different units. Programs such as Corel PHOTO-PAINT can tell you the size of an image in inches, centimetres or even millimetres. When working with computer images, though, it is often more useful to describe their size in pixels. These are dots that make up the images on your PC screen.

The number of pixels used to display Windows tells you the resolution of your screen – the more pixels there are, the more detailed the image is on screen. Most home computers are set at a resolution of 800 x 600; that's 800 pixels wide by 600 pixels tall (see Stage 2, pages 12-13).

Browse through photos on the CorelDRAW CD-ROMs and you will find pictures at many different sizes. A few might be 1024 x 768 pixels; others will be bigger, some might be smaller.

Whether it's for a special effect or just to make a picture the exact size you want, it's easy to fit a computerized picture into any space!

Distorting pictures can be fun to experiment with and will add impact to page designs.

● Wrong size pictures

Sometimes you'll want to change the size of a picture. For example, Windows lets you display a picture on screen as your Desktop background. But if you're using an 800 x 600 display and you find a 1024 x 768 pixel picture, for example, it will be too big to fit on the screen.

Programs such as PHOTO-PAINT can solve this type of problem in several ways. You

could use the selection tool to choose an 800 x 600 pixel area of the picture and then get PHOTO-PAINT to cut everything outside this area out of the picture.

In addition, you can also resize a picture to match your exact requirements, as if it has been stretched or squeezed from the edges. You can change a picture to almost any shape with PHOTO-PAINT, although this might result in distortion, as in the pictures shown above and left.

If you start with a portrait photo of 400 x 600 pixels and change it to 800 x 600 pixels, the subject's face will be stretched to twice its width. This can be fun to use for special effects. In the exercise opposite, we'll show you how to resize a picture that's too big so that it makes a better fit for the background wallpaper on your Desktop.

PC TIPS

Graphics for the Web

Resizing a picture is particularly useful when creating images for a website.
Use the exercise opposite to ensure your picture is the right size for your web page. Bear in mind when designing web pages that many visitors will be using a relatively small screen.

Fitting a picture to the Desktop

We've looked at different ways of customizing the Desktop (Stage 2, pages 10-11). Now we'll make it unique by using our own choice of picture as wallpaper.

1 Start PHOTO-PAINT and choose Open from the File menu. Insert the second CorelDRAW CD-ROM and browse through the photos to find one you'd like as your new background. We've chosen 864069.wi in the water_ani folder. Select the photo and press the Open button.

2 When a picture loads from the CD-ROM, you see a dialog box reminding you that you cannot save the picture to the CD-ROM. However, you can save it to your hard disk. Press the OK button.

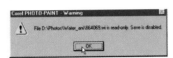

3 Now let's save the file: select the Save As option from PHOTO-PAINT's File menu. When the dialog box appears, use the Save in section to find the Windows folder. Click on the Files of type drop-down list and select BMP-Windows Bitmap. This is the format that Windows uses for Desktop wallpaper.

WHAT IT MEANS

ASPECT RATIO

The aspect ratio is the ratio of a picture's width to its height. When resizing an image, it will look distorted (squeezed or stretched) if the aspect ratio changes.

4 The first thing you'll notice is that the photo is quite large – certainly larger than your computer screen. If you were to use it as wallpaper, you wouldn't be able to see it all. But this is where PHOTO-PAINT's ability to change the size of a picture comes into effect. From the Image menu choose the Resample option.

5 From the Resample dialog box that appears you'll see that you are able to choose the exact size of the picture. Now click on the units drop-down list at the top right of the Image size selection. Select pixels from the list of options.

6 First, type 800 into the Width box. As you do so, the Height box below will automatically change to read 533 (the exact figure depends on the dimensions of your original picture – if you chose another photo, it might be different).

7 If you now try to type 600 into the Height box (the other dimension we want for this picture), you'll notice that the Width changes (it is 900 in our example). PHOTO-PAINT always tries to keep pictures in proportion when changing their size. This is because the Maintain aspect ratio box is ticked, but you can change the proportions if you want to make the picture exactly 800 x 600. First you will have to untick this box, then type in the correct Height and Width. PHOTO-PAINT will have to squeeze the photo to fit it into the width and, since 900 x 600 is enough to include most of the picture, we'll stick with this setting. Just press the OK button. Save the picture and exit CorelDRAW.

8 To make this picture your Desktop wallpaper, right-click anywhere on the Desktop to bring up the Desktop pop-up menu. Select Properties.

9 We've already used the Display Properties dialog box for changing the number of colours Windows uses (see Stage 2, pages 12-13), but you can also use it to choose pictures for the background. First click on the Background tab. This will show you a picture of what your display looks like. Press the Browse button and use the dialog box to find the file you saved in Step 3. Select it and press OK. Then press OK again to close the Display Properties dialog box.

10 The picture will instantly appear as your Windows Desktop background wallpaper.

PHOTO-PAINT's different brushes

Artists who work with acrylic or water-based paints have a variety of different brush styles available to them. With PHOTO-PAINT, computer artists have just as much choice.

One of the major benefits that CorelDRAW PHOTO-PAINT has over simple paint programs is the amount of control it gives you over brush types. You can choose from a huge range of brushes, brush nib shapes, and the type of 'paint' that is used.

You're not restricted to painting on perfectly smooth paper, either. You can choose the type of surface on which you are painting – such as cartridge paper or an expensive cotton canvas, as used by real artists to heighten the reality of the paint surface.

● **Choosing your brushes**
When you click on the Paint Tool button in the toolbox, you will see PHOTO-PAINT's Property Bar change to reflect the options available (below). These options let you choose the type of brush – from conventional brushes to pencils, airbrushes and even specialist brushes that mimic famous painting

styles, such as Impressionism and Pointillism. Some of the other popular options available include quick access to choice of brush size and nib shape (whether circular or square) directly from the Property Bar.

For full control over the huge variety of available brushes, you use the program's Docker windows. Like CorelDRAW, PHOTO-PAINT brings together related options into a single window. Corel calls these options Dockers because they 'dock' into position at the side of the PHOTO-PAINT window.

● **Brushes and Nibs**
Select Brush Settings from the Window menu's Dockers sub-menu. At the far right is the usual X button for closing the window, and in

When you are using the Paint Tool, the Property Bar changes to give you quick access to many brush choices.

The canvas effect can be used to make a photograph (top) look as though it's been painted on one of the materials used by artists, such as cotton (above), wood, paper or canvas.

the middle is the Roll-Up button. Click on this to make the contents of the window appear or disappear.

The main part of the Brush Settings Docker menu lets you choose from a wide variety of ready-made nib shapes and sizes. Here you'll find more than the simple circular and square options offered on the Property Bar. For example, there are stars, swirls, and even a collection of unusual shapes for a paintbrush, such as lions, birds and human figures. When you click on one of these, painting becomes as simple as choosing a colour and clicking on the painting area you wish to fill in.

If you can't find the nib shape you want, you can create your own. Anything you can draw with the mouse can be made into a nib. This is one area of painting that is easier to do on a computer than with a real brush.

● Effects

As well as changing the properties of the brush, you can also change the type of paint you use. This is achieved via the Effects menu, which allows you to alter the thickness, 'wetness' and texture of the paint.

Effects work slightly differently from the brush options. When you alter the type of brush and nib, it affects the things you paint subsequently – your existing painting remains as it was before. When you use Effects, however, it affects your existing painting. For example, if you select part of your picture and use the Effects menu to add a wet paint look, it will affect only the selected area.

● Canvas effects

With all the options possible for the brushes and paint, it's no surprise that PHOTO-PAINT also allows you to alter the background of your 'paper' as well. This is done by using canvas filters, which can be added at any stage of your drawing to give a texture to the background.

If you want to give your picture the look of a painting created on canvas, for example, you simply apply a linen-type texture to the whole painting area. You can have lots of fun with your existing pictures by applying effects to them. For example, if you have a photograph of a relative, you can make it look like a painted image just by making use of a canvas effect. No extra painting work is necessary and when printed out on high-quality paper, you have an ideal gift!

Advanced Paint Tool Settings

IN ADDITION to changing the nib and brush types, you can also make a number of alterations to the way the brushstrokes are applied to the page.

At first, these will seem like minor changes, mostly because you simply have to change a percentage or move a slider bar. But they can have a profound effect on how your brush appears on the page.

You can access the brush options through the different sections of the Brush Settings Docker. The top part lets you change the angle of the brush and its size.

By clicking on the small black arrows next to each section name, you reveal extra settings for the Paint Tool.

The Brush Texture section includes options for the way brushstrokes bleed into a painting. For example, you can simulate watercolour painting by tweaking the Bleed and Sustain Color settings so that as you paint in one colour, it blends with the colours of paint already there underneath.

The Dab Attributes option lets you control the way successive dabs of the brush are applied. You can change the spacing – making brushstrokes closer together or further apart, depending on your specific needs – and you can also add some subtle (and not so subtle) colour variations by moving the Hue Saturation and Lightness sliders away from their normal '0' settings.

Choosing brushes and paint effects

To get the best out of your own abilities (and those of your computer) try using the different brush styles PHOTO-PAINT has on offer. We look at some here.

1 Start a new picture and then click on the Paint Tool from the toolbox on the left of the PHOTO-PAINT screen.

2 Select Brush Settings (far right) from the Dockers sub-menu on the Window menu (right).

3 Use the pop-up window's scroll bar to look through the different nibs. Pick one that would be useful for drawing a tree and single-click on it.

4 Now select a shade of green from the colour palette on the right and start to paint a tree. Feel free to experiment with different nibs for the trunk.

5 For the second tree we shall use the same nib, but alter the texture of the paint so that it looks as if it has been applied wet. Start by painting a second tree next to the first.

6 Select the Rectangular Mask Tool from the toolbox and drag a rectangle over the second tree so that it completely encompasses it.

7 From the Effects menu, select Distort and then choose the Wet Paint option.

8 A dialog box appears, with two sliders to control the effect. Alter the size of the drips (Percent) and the wetness of the paint (Wetness), and you can see your picture change to show the effects. Click the OK button when you are happy with it.

9 For the final tree, try one of the pre-set brush types. Click on the Art Brush button (inset below) on the far left of the Property Bar and select the last brush. Then select Pointillism from the drop-down list box just to its right.

10 Now, as you paint your tree, you will find that it is built up from many small dots. However, the great thing is that you don't have to draw the individual dots yourself, as PHOTO-PAINT does it for you.

Making your own brush nibs

As you can see, there are many different ways you can alter your chosen brush in PHOTO-PAINT. If you still can't find exactly what you want, you can make your own.

AS WELL AS customizing the brushes by using pre-set commands, you can also create a custom nib completely from scratch. In fact, the pre-set nibs are really just simple bitmap pictures, so you can easily create your own and specify it as a nib. Below we do just that by drawing a picture of a leaf and then using it to paint a tree.

When drawing a new nib bitmap, you should remember that it will generally be used with one colour at a time. Any holes you wish to include in the nib bitmap drawing will also have to be carefully drawn to ensure they have no gaps in them through which the brush fill colour might seep.

When making any customization alterations to the nibs, it is best to do it at a high zoom magnification because most brush nibs are, by necessity, fairly small when they appear on-screen.

1 Start a new painting and create a simple shape with the Paint Tool. Take extra care to make sure the shape is clear and distinct. In our example we've used a leaf.

2 Draw a Rectangle Mask around your design. Now select Create from Contents of Mask from the menu that appears when you check the Nib Options button.

3 Click OK in the box that appears (below) and the shape you want to use will immediately become a nib.

4 Use your new nib to paint a picture. Notice how the black and white areas of your original nib control where the paint is applied.

5 Go to the Brush Settings window and click the Brush Texture heading. Change the Bleed setting to 50. Now use a star-shaped brush and drag it to create some fireworks.

6 Use the Dab Attributes section to adjust the way successive dabs appear. Experiment with the Spacing, Spread and the settings. See how the star brush paints differently.

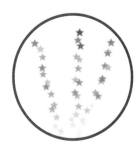

7 By using these settings wisely, you can come up with many natural-looking effects that would otherwise take a long time to create, such as flocks of birds, with a single stroke.

Being creative with PHOTO-PAINT's filters

Even if you're no good at painting with the mouse, you can use PHOTO-PAINT's many filters to edit and customize existing images so that you can create your own works of art.

Despite having the help of PHOTO-PAINT'S huge number of brushes and nibs, not everyone is cut out to be a computer artist. Painting with a mouse needs just the same creative and compositional skills as painting with real brushes and genuine oils or watercolours. The mouse and PHOTO-PAINT's many powerful features are no substitute for talent.

However, the companies that make graphics programs know that not everyone is a latent Van Gogh, so they pack plenty of features into their products to help make PC art relatively easy. In fact, many of the professional computer artists who buy advanced art programs, such as PHOTO-PAINT, don't intend to paint images from scratch. Instead they want to apply their programs' image-editing features to work on existing images.

● Filter features
By being creative with the dozens of powerful filters built into PHOTO-PAINT, you can manipulate any type of picture. Photo-retouching filters (see pages 78-79) let you adjust brightness, contrast and the amount of highlights, mid-tones and shadows in an image. Every media art department in the world uses such filters to make photos as clear as possible before publication.

Other filters have much more dramatic effects. You can apply PHOTO-PAINT's Squizz filter to warp a picture (see page 88). The effect is like looking through a distorting glass lens: as with all the filters, you can add as much distortion as you like and control which parts of the picture are changed.

CorelDRAW's filters can turn your photograph into a Pointillist 'masterpiece' or a shimmering reflection.

These filters are a great way to get youngsters interested in the world of computer image editing. It's fun to take photos of mum or dad and stretch their faces into crazy shapes. You can save the photo and print it out on a colour printer to make a unique personalized greetings card.

● Instant artist
If you want to create the illusion of a painted image, PHOTO-PAINT's filters can help out. There is a special set called Art Strokes, that can turn any photo into a painting style of your choice (see opposite).

At first glance, the Art Strokes seem similar to the texture effects that PHOTO-PAINT can apply to an image (see page 83). By adding a texture to a photo, you can give the impression that it is printed on a surface, such as canvas, linen or even concrete. It's a great effect, but the image still

PAINTING MADE EASY

By applying the Watercolor Art Strokes filter to a photograph, such as a row of trees, you can transform the photo into a stunning graphic that has the appearance of a watercolour painting, as shown below.

looks like a photo. By contrast, the Art Strokes filters are much more sophisticated and much more flexible. They actually repaint the whole picture by applying brush strokes to a plain background.

The idea behind filter software is that it looks at the colours of the pixels in the original photo and uses them to choose paint colours. It then repaints the picture in a variety of different styles. For example, it can redraw the picture as if it were created with watercolours: the filter picks up the main colours from the photo, but when it creates the new picture, it simulates the delicacy of watercolour brush strokes to give the typical wash effect of watercolour pictures. The original picture is hardly recognizable, as all the tiny details are washed out, leaving a more artistic version of the image (see Painting made easy box, opposite page).

● **Customizing tools**

There's almost always a lot more subtlety and flexibility in these effects than in the simpler texture ones. You can see just how the filter will affect your image and fine tune it in many different ways. For example, in the Palette Knife filter, you can change the size of the knife itself, alter its angle or soften the edge of the paint stroke laid down by the knife.

Combining filters

PHOTO-PAINT's filters needn't be used in isolation – you can combine them to get even better effects.

To create a particularly realistic painting effect from a photograph, you can combine several filters in succession. For example, if you use the Impressionist Art Stroke filter (see page 89) and then the Canvas texture, you can turn a flat photograph into an image that looks like it has been painted on coarse fabric.

You're not restricted to realistic images – there are plenty of weird and wacky filters that can help you to create out-of-this-world images from your photos. For example, the Psychedelic command (in the Color Transform sub-menu) lets you create the wild colour changes that you often see in pop videos. You can then use this with other filters to change the original beyond all recognition.

You can also use different filters on different parts of your image. Just select an area before choosing a filter from the Effects menu. Applying different filters to separate areas of an image is perfect for creating a composite look. You could, for example, create a 'painting' done half in oils and half in watercolours.

The starting point for many a graphic adventure using PHOTO-PAINT's filters is an ordinary photograph.

Use the Impressionist Art Strokes filter and you can turn the photo into an Impressionist-style painting.

Next, use the Canvas texture to make the picture look even more like a real painting.

This pool-side photo has had the Psychedelic filter applied to it, brightening its contrasts and colours.

Next, use the Ripple filter to add a watery look to the psychedelic pool-side graphic.

Turn a single photo into an amazing composite painting, using as many filters as you need.

Fun with photos and filters

Have fun with PHOTO-PAINT. Here we attack a portrait with the Squizz filter.

1 Start PHOTO-PAINT and open a portrait photograph. We've opted for 871014.wi from the People folder on the third of CorelDRAW's CD-ROMs, but you can use any image you have to hand.

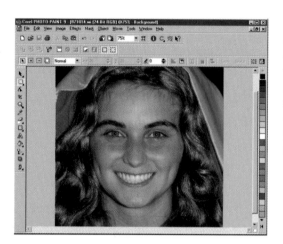

2 Click the Effects menu and then select SQUIZZ 1.5 from the HSoft sub-menu. When the Squizz welcome screen appears, click the BRUSH button at the bottom of the screen.

3 Your picture now appears on the left of the dialog box, with settings on the right. As your mouse passes over the picture, a circular outline shows the Squizz brush. If necessary, you can change the size of this brush in the Brush Properties section of the dialog box.

4 To start Squizzing, drag the brush over any part of the portrait. Squizz drags the paint around as if it is made of elastic. Notice how the colours are still as smoothly blended as in the original photo.

5 When you've finished distorting your portrait, click the Apply button on the right to make these changes to your photo (or click Cancel to leave the photo as it is).

6 Squizz has two modes of working. The first is the brush you've already been using. The second is the Grid option, which helps create regular distortions. Open another photo and bring up Squizz again, this time clicking the Grid button when the welcome screen appears. The image appears with a rectangular grid overlying the picture (inset).

7 Click and drag the corners where the lines intersect. When you release the mouse button, Squizz squeezes and stretches the pixels in the image to match the new shape of the grid.

8 You can move as many of the corners as you like, gradually warping the image into a new shape. When you click the Apply button, PHOTO-PAINT makes the changes to your image. It's a great way to see a new slant on familiar images.

PC TIPS

If you know what sort of distorting shape you want to make with the grid, you can drag as many of the corners as quickly as you like. Once you stop, PHOTO-PAINT will catch up and redraw the preview with your changes shown.

Paintings from photographs

Create a painting by using PHOTO-PAINT's Art Strokes on a photograph.

1 Open an existing photograph in PHOTO-PAINT. Select a picture that has very distinct shapes and outlines, such as this image of a pyramid. Click on Art Strokes in the Effects menu and select the Sketch Pad command from the sub-menu.

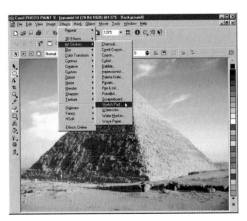

2 As soon as the dialog box appears, PHOTO-PAINT applies the Sketch Pad filter to the image. It uses the default settings for this particular filter. In a few moments you see a black-and-white shaded sketch of your photograph.

3 The settings that give you control over the virtual pencil that PHOTO-PAINT has used are in the Sketch Pad dialog box. Try dragging the Style slider right to the Fine end and doing the same with the Outline slider.

4 Your sketched photo is redrawn, with lots more detail added by the pencil. This shows the rough texture of the pyramid faces more clearly than the original Sketch Pad settings.

5 PHOTO-PAINT also has a virtual set of coloured pencils up its sleeve: click the Color option in the dialog box to access them. Make the sketch, then click the OK button when you are happy with the effect.

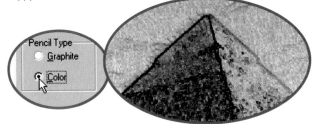

6 PHOTO-PAINT is packed with great instant-art filters: open the photo again and try the Impressionist filter, listed in the Art Strokes menu. You get a superb result within a few seconds; painting this with a mouse would challenge even the best computer artist's abilities.

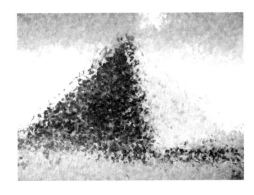

PC TIPS

To view both the original photo and the altered picture, click the button with the two rectangles that appears on the dialog box's title bar. This will show the images side by side.

7 For a different Impressionist effect, select the Dabs option in the Impressionist dialog box. You can add more colours to the Impressionist palette by dragging the Coloration setting to the right.

Using CorelDRAW to combine photographs and drawings is lots of fun and very easy. It's a great chance to be really creative and makes use of the advanced facilities of this program.

Adding photos to drawings

The real beauty of the CorelDRAW package is that it contains programs for creating and editing both bitmap images (such as photos and paintings) and vector images (such as drawings and illustrations). You'll be able to get even more out of the program, however, once you learn how to combine these two types of images. CorelDRAW makes it easy.

CorelDRAW itself is a drawing program (see Stage 2, pages 70-71) and Corel PHOTO-PAINT is a bitmap editor (see pages 74-77). So far, we've kept the two areas separate, but CorelDRAW can also use bitmap images created in other programs. It also lets you use bitmap pictures as patterns to fill objects in your drawings.

● More realism
Although you can create accurate pictures with CorelDRAW, nothing is as realistic as a photograph. And there are many occasions when using a bitmap image is preferable to using vectors, as CorelDRAW does.

Greetings cards, for example, can benefit from the personal touch. While you could simply use a photo editor to create and print

a bitmap picture, by using the picture in a drawing, you can add words and shapes in a manner that is not possible when you are using a photo editor.

The added benefit of importing bitmaps to your drawings is that you can edit them in the same way as vector objects. You can change the appearance of the picture and add special 2D and 3D effects. The possibilities are limited only by your imagination.

● Adding a bitmap to your drawing
The actual process of adding a bitmap picture to a drawing is easy. Browse through the CD-ROMs that came with CorelDRAW. One of them is stuffed full of photographs that you can use for any purpose. Remember, the manual shows small preview pictures of the images on the CD-ROM to help you find what you're looking for.

Once you've found a suitable picture, you can simply drag and drop it on to your drawing. In the following example, we'll create a composite picture using a photograph and some CorelDRAW shapes. We'll also show how to use a bitmap pattern to fill a CorelDRAW shape.

PC TIPS

It's best to run Windows in 24-bit colour mode (see Stage 2, pages 12-13) when using a graphics program such as CorelDRAW. This is because pictures look best when there are plenty of colours available to display them. If you would like to use a photo that contains thousands of colours, trying to display it on a computer that is set up to show only 256 colours at once will result in a poor on-screen image.

Making a composite image

CorelDRAW can combine drawings with photos. Here we use some of the images from the CorelDRAW CD-ROM.

1 Adding a photo to a vector drawing is very simple in CorelDRAW. For this example, we'll add a photograph to a frame. CorelDRAW has some ready-made frames in its clip art collection, so we'll start by clicking on the Tools menu and selecting the Clipart option from the Scrapbook sub-menu.

2 Choose a border from the second CorelDRAW CD-ROM. This one is in the Africa folder. You can load it into CorelDRAW simply by double-clicking on the icon.

3 You'll see the frame appear on your page. You can now add a photo to use in the frame. Insert the third CorelDRAW CD-ROM. Choose Photos from the Scrapbook sub-menu.

4 Again, the choice of photo is up to you. Here, we've used 865067.wi, which is in the Ani_king folder within the Photos folder. Add the photo by dragging and dropping it on to the frame.

5 To put the photograph behind the frame, click on it with the right mouse button, click on the Order options and select the To Back command. In this respect, the photograph you have added works just like any other object you would add to a picture.

6 The photo is a little large for the border, so we need to make it fit into the frame correctly. Now that it's behind the frame, we can use the Shape Tool (inset, below) to grab each corner of the picture and take it to the inside corner of the picture frame.

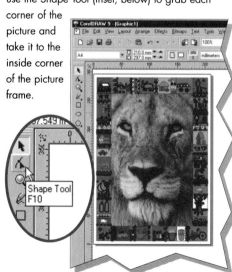

Filling shapes with bitmap patterns

1 You can add bitmap patterns to any shape in your drawings. For this example, just start with a new shape. We've used the Polygon Tool to draw a simple pentagon. Click on the newly drawn shape with the right mouse button and select Properties from the pop-up menu that appears.

2 Click on the Fill tab of the dialog box that appears. From the line of six buttons, click the third from the left and select Bitmap from the list of Pattern fill options.

3 Click on the drop-down palette of bitmaps and choose one of the patterns. Press the Apply button and the bitmap pattern will fill the entire polygon.

Hardware

Adding more memory

Adding more memory is one of the easiest and least expensive upgrades you can make to your computer – and it can also be one of the most effective.

It's easy to think of your PC as a single box, much like a video recorder or a CD player. However, unlike a video or a CD player – which you tamper with at your peril – a PC is built to be upgradable (see Stage 2, pages 110-111).

There are two reasons you might want to upgrade your computer: to add new functions and capabilities (adding a larger monitor or plugging in a scanner, for example) or to make your PC work faster.

● Upgrading for performance

We've already covered some examples of adding new devices (see Stage 2, 104-107 and 108-109); here, we'll look at improving your PC's performance. It's a fact of computing life that once you've bought a PC,

newer, faster models will hit the shops within months. It's also true that new software often works more slowly than previous versions because of all its new features. It's not unusual to find that upgrading your software seems to make your computer run slower! To counter this performance problem, you can change or add individual components

inside your computer. For example, changing to a better graphics card will make the software that uses it run faster. Without a doubt though, the best way to make your computer run much faster is to add more Random Access Memory (RAM) – and in all cases, the more the merrier.

● More memory

Windows likes memory – the more you've got, the more easily Windows can make space for the huge number of programs and files it uses. Many home computers were initially sold with 32MB of RAM. This seems plenty – it's enough to store 33,554,432 bytes (see Stage 1, pages 96-97). However, many programs (including Windows) can use up many millions of bytes. When Windows runs out of memory for the programs and documents it is using, it stores them temporarily on the hard disk. You might notice your computer's hard disk light flashing from time to time, even when you're not opening or saving programs or documents on the hard disk. This is a sign that

Here you can see how much faster a computer goes when more memory is added to its existing 16MB. The yellow bar shows the computer before adding memory, while the red, blue and green bars show the improvement with different amounts of memory.

SIMMs, DIMMs

Short for single and dual inline memory module, respectively, these are tiny circuit boards containing memory chips. They plug into matching slots on the PC's motherboard. Most PCs use either SIMMs or DIMMs, although a few can use both. Your PC's manual should tell you which your PC uses.

Windows is swapping information between the memory and the computer's hard disk.

Unfortunately, the hard disk is much slower than the RAM memory and swapping the information from one to the other is also a slow process. With more memory – 64MB or even 128MB – Windows has to do much less of this swapping, so its programs run more quickly and smoothly.

● Memory costs

Memory is the most cost-effective upgrade you can buy. Adding another 16MB to a computer which has only 16MB fitted can increase performance by 17 per cent, and should cost around £45. However, due to the volatile nature of the computer business, the price is subject to fluctuation. As memory is

RAM memory comes in strips called SIMMs and DIMMs and is simple to install, but it is fragile and should be handled only by an experienced technician.

supplied on SIMM or DIMM modules, adding memory is a simple, and therefore cheap, upgrade. Since computers normally have several slots for memory modules, you can sometimes add more without replacing your existing modules. It's still worth getting a dealer or computer expert to add more memory, as it's important to get exactly the right type (see Fitting the right type of memory, below).

Try to track down a local dealer who either builds systems or does repairs – he may charge a little more for the memory than the big mail order firms that advertise in the magazines, but he will probably fit it free of charge.

How much memory you can add depends on how many free memory module slots there are on the motherboard. Older computers often have four SIMM slots on the motherboard. SIMMs must be fitted in matching pairs: two 8MB SIMMs for 16MB or four 16MB SIMMs for 64MB, for example. If there are empty SIMM slots, the dealer can use these to upgrade your memory, but if all four are used, upgrading memory means discarding the current SIMMs with

higher capacity modules (the dealer may accept these in part exchange). Newer PCs use DIMM slots – typically two or three. One of the main advantages of DIMMs is that they can be added singly. So if your PC has two 16MB DIMMs and one spare DIMM slot you can add another 64MB DIMM to take the total RAM up to 96MB.

● No software installation

One of the best aspects of adding more memory compared to other computer add-ons is that there's no extra software to install or set up after the new memory has been added. Windows uses the extra memory straight away so that each and every one of your programs can work more efficiently.

Here we can see two vacant slots for memory modules on the motherboard.

Here are the same two slots with two 32MB memory modules fitted in position.

FITTING THE RIGHT TYPE OF MEMORY

We don't recommend that you try fitting new RAM yourself. This is partly because it's easy to cause irreparable damage – for example, it's all too easy to destroy memory chips with static electricity – and partly because it's just as easy to get the wrong kind of memory module.

There is a vast array of different types of memory and this can be very confusing. Fitting the wrong kind of memory module could damage the memory, your computer – or both.

You will see many abbreviations used in adverts: FPM RAM, EDO RAM, SDRAM, PC100 and so on. You might also see references to parity and non-parity. All this jargon refers to the various different ways that the memory chips work.

Until a few years ago, FPM memory was used in all computers. However, more recent types of memory, such as EDO RAM and SDRAM, have been adopted because they work faster than FPM

RAM. If your computer will accept it, it is best to buy SDRAM type memory.

SDRAM chips are the latest type of chips and are commonly used in PCs that use DIMM slots. Despite these chips being so new, the fast pace of PC development means that there are several different variants. These subtle variations are based on the speed that the PC's motherboard operates.

For example, for motherboards that run at 66MHz, 66MHz DIMMs are required. Similarly, there are 100MHz DIMMs (known as PC100 DIMMs), and 133MHz DIMMs (known as PC133 DIMMs). Generally speaking, the faster the chips run, the more expensive they are.

Your computer's manual should tell you which types of memory your computer can work with, but a computer dealer will be better able to check the type your computer is fitted with and, if necessary, fit a similar type.

Screen space is always at a premium on a computer. Windows itself takes up a large amount of space with its Taskbar and Start menu, while programs, such as Word, also use up space with their menus and toolbars. The simplest solution to the space problem is a bigger monitor.

The first benefit you'll get is more screen area, which means the objects on the screen are easier to see and can be used at a bigger size. More importantly, larger monitors can run at a higher resolution than standard 14- or 15-inch monitors. This means that small text will be more readable and pictures will be both clearer and more detailed. One way in which the extra resolution can help is that, with the extra detail, you can see two documents side by side and easily

Upgrading to a 17-inch monitor

Change to a bigger monitor and you'll get more information on screen. These pictures represent the difference, in both size and detail, between a 14-inch monitor (top) and a 17-inch monitor (above).

WHAT IT MEANS

REFRESH RATE

Monitors work by drawing the image as a series of lines one after the other, from top to bottom. The speed at which this is done is called the refresh rate, and the faster it is, the better the image looks. If the refresh rate is too slow, the screen appears to flicker. This can lead to headaches.

Many new computers are supplied with a 14- or 15-inch monitor, but there's much to be gained from buying a larger one.

copy and paste information from one to the other.

We've used two screen images to demonstrate the difference between two resolutions (left). The top picture shows 800 x 600 pixels – a common setting used on 14- and 15-inch monitors; the bottom picture shows 1024 x 768, common for monitors one size bigger – 17-inch.

You can increase the resolution on any monitor, but it's unlikely that a 14- or 15-inch monitor will work very well at any resolution higher than 800 x 600 pixels. Some will try to show 1024 x 768 pixels, but text, icons and toolbar buttons appear very small without the extra screen size to show them. In addition, some 14- and 15-inch monitors can show a resolution

of only 1024 x 768 at a low refresh rate. If you really want to work at high resolutions, you will need a larger monitor. There are various sizes, but the next after the 15-inch is

MEASURING MONITORS

Like TVs, monitors are measured across the screen diagonally. However, if you measure any monitor screen, you'll find that it's actually around an inch or so smaller than claimed. This is true for all screens except those built into laptop computers, which reflect the true measure of the screen diagonal. When looking at advertisements for monitors, look for 'Viewable Area' or 'Viewable Image Size' figures – these are the true measures of monitor size.

the 17-inch. There are also monitors in the 19- to 21-inch range, but these are mainly aimed at professional computer users. Some of these large monitors are much more expensive. In addition, the longer cathode ray tube takes up a lot of space and is usually too long to fit conveniently on most desktops.

A 17-inch monitor is therefore a good compromise between size and cost; you can expect to pick one up for between £150 and £300. It's still a substantial purchase, but it is one that will last for many years. Even when you decide you want to replace your computer, you can carry on using your 17-inch monitor with the new system unit you purchase.

Installing a new monitor should prove no problem, as it has only two connecting cables – one for power and the other for carrying the signal from the computer's graphics card. Both of these will be supplied with the monitor.

MONITOR DETECTION

If Windows doesn't detect your new monitor automatically, don't worry. Check the material that came with the monitor and you should find a floppy disk. This contains computer data files that ensure that Windows knows how to get the best from your new monitor. If there's no floppy disk and no mention of how to set the monitor up correctly, call your supplier or the maker's helpline.

Installing a new monitor

Larger monitors enable you to see more information, more clearly. Here we show you how to make your computing easier on the eye.

1 The first thing to do when installing a new monitor is to remove the old one. Before doing so, make sure that both the monitor and computer are turned off and the power cord is unplugged. That done, unplug the signal cable from the socket on the back of your computer. The cable might be screwed into place, so you will need to unscrew it before pulling it out.

2 Here you can see the difference in screen size between the old and new monitors (the old monitor is in the background). You might also notice that your new monitor is much deeper than the old one. This is because the cathode ray tube used to display the image needs to be longer. As a general rule, the depth of monitors increases with their screen size, so considerable allowances need to be made for monitors with screens over 21 inches in size. You will also realize that the new monitor is heavier than the old one and so you might need help lifting it onto the desk.

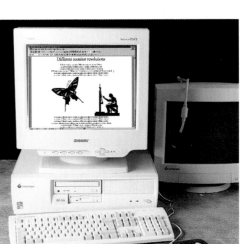

3 Connect the new cables in exactly the same way as the ones on the old monitor were connected. Remember to use the screws that secure the signal cable to the graphics card socket to ensure a firm and reliable connection. You can now plug in the power cable and turn on your computer and monitor.

4 Most new monitors are automatically detected by Windows, and as a result you will see messages appear on screen. You now need to tell Windows to use a higher resolution. Click the right-hand mouse button on an empty part of the Desktop and select Properties from the pop-up menu.

5 When the Display Properties dialog box appears, click on the Settings tab. You will see a slider that allows you to change the size of the screen: click on the slider and drag it until 1024 by 768 pixels is shown. Press the OK button and Windows will change the screen to the new resolution.

Adding a Zip drive

Zip drives have been around for only a few years but they are now firmly established as a popular form of computer storage. And it's easy to see why.

Zip disks resemble a chunky floppy disk but they can take up to 100MB or 250MB of information – 70 to 170 times more than an ordinary floppy. The drives cost between £90 and £150, while a 100MB disk costs around £8. The disks are also reusable, which means you can save and erase data as many times as you wish, just as you would with a regular floppy disk.

● **Convenient storage**
Zip disks are conveniently portable, too. You can easily fit two or three into a shirt pocket or bag, and the drive itself isn't a great deal bigger (about the size of a paperback book).

If your computer is starting to fill up with files, or you're worried about losing data, why not add a Zip drive? For a small outlay and very little bother, you'll instantly gain lots of extra storage.

A Zip drive is a simple, plug-in device, while its high-capacity disks (right) are only a little larger than a conventional floppy.

In stark comparison to just about every other PC peripheral ever made, the Zip drive is quite a stylish addition to your desktop. Add all that up and you've got a very affordable, handy and desirable computer add-on.

In office use, the main function of Zip disks is to send big files from one place to another; at 100MB or 250MB each, they can take a lot of data – the text of several lengthy books, for example. But Zip disks have plenty of appeal for home computer users, too. They are very effective for backing up data (see box, left), being far bigger and far faster than the now old-fashioned floppies. You'd need 70 floppies to provide the same storage space as a 100MB Zip disk. Also, Zip disks are far more physically robust and less prone to magnetic corruption.

● **A choice of drives**
Zip drives come in various formats. The best type to buy as an add-on is an external type, which is connected to the computer by a cable. External Zip drives come in three versions.

A parallel port Zip drive connects to any PC via the parallel port socket. The SCSI (pronounced 'scuzzy') version needs a special SCSI connector, which typically takes the form of a card that plugs into a spare slot inside your PC and gives you a new socket at the back. The USB Zip Drive plugs into your PC's USB (Universal Serial Bus) socket.

ZIP DISK BACKUPS

While transferring data between computers might be the most common use of Zip disks, they also work extremely well as backup disks. Using Microsoft Backup (see Stage 2, pages 24-25) you simply work your way through the Wizard-style interface, choose the files, folders or entire drives you want to back up, and then select your Zip drive as the destination. If you're backing up a large amount of data, the software will simply prompt you to insert another disk when the current one is full. The software automatically splits large files across a number of disks (see below), so the process is almost entirely automatic.

It's so quick and easy that anyone with a Zip-equipped PC has no excuse for not performing regular backups.

When you've connected the drive and started the PC, the Zip drive icon will appear in the My Computer window. Its drive letter will depend on the devices fitted.

The main advantages of external Zip drives, whether parallel, SCSI or USB, are that they are a cinch to install and very portable. If you want to transfer big files to another computer which doesn't have a Zip, you can just take the drive along as well as the disk. A SCSI Zip drive is a lot faster than a parallel port one, but SCSI cards are tricky to install. The USB drive has the advantage of being 'hot-pluggable' – you can connect it without switching off your PC. You can also get an internal Zip drive, which occupies a 3½-inch bay at the front of your PC – the same size as a floppy drive. These tend to be a bit cheaper and will reduce the clutter on your desktop. But they aren't portable and can be quite tricky to install. You really need to get a professional to fit an internal drive – which, of course, negates the saving over an external model.

● Using a Zip drive

Once your drive is installed (and, in the case of an external type, turned on), you can access it straight from the Desktop in the same way as for a floppy or CD-ROM drive. (You should always plug in the external drive before turning on the PC.)

The Zip drive icon will simply appear inside your My Computer folder, where it will automatically be assigned the next letter of the alphabet (following those used by devices such as your hard disk and CD-ROM drive) as its drive letter.

PC TIPS

The original Zip drive does not have an on/off switch, so you must remember to unplug it after use to turn it off. Newer ZipPlus drives have an on/off switch and a smaller, more portable power unit. This is compatible with the original drive and can be bought separately.

Installing an external, parallel port Zip drive

Connecting this type of Zip drive takes a matter of minutes, but don't forget to switch the PC off before you begin and then restart afterwards.

1 The Zip drive attaches to your computer's parallel port – if you already have a printer attached to this port, disconnect it.

2 Connect the cable from the Zip drive to the parallel port, then tighten the plug's two security screws.

3 If you had to disconnect your printer in Step 1, connect it to the parallel port on the back of the Zip drive.

4 Plug the Zip drive's power adaptor into the mains and connect the small power cable to the side of the Zip drive.

5 Switch on the power to the computer. Windows will detect the Zip drive. Follow the on-screen instructions – make sure you have your Windows CD-ROM and the Zip drive's setup disk to hand.

6 Once installation is complete, you can insert a Zip disk and copy files to and from it by using Windows' normal drag and drop procedures.

Computer cameras

Digital cameras are the latest computer accessories to find their way into people's pockets. A few years ago digital cameras cost over £1,000, but now a basic model sells at less than £200. So what do you get for your money?

A digital camera is similar to a traditional film-based camera, except that it stores your pictures electronically – that is, in a digital format that your PC can then use. Both traditional and digital cameras use a lens to focus the picture, an aperture to control how much light enters into the camera, and a shutter to control how long the light comes into the camera for. But that's where the similarities end.

In a film-based camera, the picture is projected onto a piece of plastic film with a light-sensitive coating. But in a digital camera, the picture is

Imagine a camera that requires no film, has no processing costs, lets you send photographs around the world within a few minutes of taking the shot and even allows you to re-touch the photograph using your computer. All this is possible with a digital camera.

Some digital cameras like the Agfa 780c (centre) look like conventional cameras but, as well as a viewfinder, the camera has a screen on the back showing the picture you have captured. Others, like the Kodak DC3400 and Canon PowerShot S20, have more distinct styling.

projected onto an electronic component called a charge-coupled device (CCD) that scans and converts the image into an electronic data file.

● Colour by numbers
The file consists of numbers that represent the colour and brightness of all the spots that make up the picture. This information is then stored in memory – like the memory in your PC – inside the camera.

Photographic film needs to be processed and developed. Firstly, the film is chemically 'fixed' so that light does not affect it any further. And secondly, the pictures on the film are stored as negatives and have to be printed onto special photographic paper. Although this can be done in as little as an hour, it's not cheap and it requires a laboratory.

With a digital camera, you simply connect it to your PC and 'download' the digital pictures. Transferring the pictures to your computer is quick and costs nothing, although if you print them with your colour printer, you have to pay for the paper and coloured inks.

● Private view
Many digital cameras include a built-in liquid crystal display (LCD) that allows you to view a picture as soon as you take it. This means that if you don't like it, you just erase it from the camera's memory and shoot it again.

If your digital camera has a viewing screen, you can check the picture as soon as you have taken it. Then, if you don't like the result, you can simply erase it.

Later, with the appropriate software, you can view the pictures instantly on your computer monitor.

For example, let's say you want to send a favourite aunt in Australia the latest family photos. Simply point your camera at the clan and shoot – within a fraction of a second, the picture is taken.

● Automatic settings

Like most 35mm cameras, everything is automatic, but it can take a little time for a digital camera to work out the light settings and automatically adjust the aperture size and shutter

After installing the software supplied, the pictures can be downloaded onto a PC for viewing or printing. Each of them can be viewed in 'thumbnail' form (above). You can zoom in on any individual frame to see it in more detail (right). Some programs include extensive features for display, editing and printing out – as well as for changing the camera settings.

CHECKPOINT ✔

Here are some of the key features of digital cameras that you should consider before buying one:

☑ Resolution: the number of dots making up the image. The higher the resolution, the better. Very cheap (approximately £100) digital cameras may have a resolution as low as 640 x 480, while for mid-range, pricier models you should be looking for 1024 x 768 as a minimum resolution.

☑ Image storage: the number of pictures the camera will store. On many cameras you can store more images if you choose a lower (worse) resolution. Standard storage ranges are around 50–200 pictures at low resolution (640 x 480 or thereabouts) and 5-20 pictures at maximum resolution.

☑ Memory cards: Nearly all digital cameras let you plug in a credit card-sized memory card to store extra images. Check the capacity and price of these additional cards.

☑ Review panel: Nearly all digital cameras feature an LCD panel where you can check if the picture has come out correctly. Such panels are relatively small; others fold out to give a larger viewing area.

speed. Then there may be a further four to eight-second delay while the camera converts the photograph into a digital format. If your digital camera has a built-in LCD preview screen and you see, for example, that one of the family members wasn't smiling, you can simply erase the photo from the memory and take it again!

● Downloading

When you've taken your quota of photos, or the camera's memory is full, it's time to transfer your snaps to your PC. To do this, simply plug the lead supplied into the camera, then plug the other end into your computer (see pages 102-103). You can then run the software supplied and transfer the photos.

Once the photos are copied to your computer, you can erase the originals from the camera and start shooting

ARE THEY AS GOOD AS THE REAL THING?

Yes and no...
If you're looking for award-winning, high-quality printed photographs, then a digital camera does not meet the same standards as a film-based camera. First, photographic film can record much more detail than even the best digital cameras. Digital pictures can sometimes appear rather 'fuzzy' when studied closely.

Second, the lenses fitted to most digital cameras are not as good as those on conventional cameras. This degrades the final image. Only the most sophisticated digital cameras have lenses as good as those on film-based cameras. But if you're looking for photos that are adequate for a range of jobs, perhaps for a newsletter, advertisement, photo-ID or to send a picture by e-mail to a family member or friend, then a digital camera is ideal. There are no film or development costs, and you can duplicate the photographs by copying a file on your computer.

again. In the meantime, the photographs can be viewed on your computer. If you have a colour printer, you will be able to print copies – remembering that the higher the resolution of the printer, the better the quality of the printout.

Because the pictures are digital, you can even edit them with a graphics package. For example, you could brush out that spot on your nose or even copy the spot to a less deserving family member!

Also, if you have access to the Internet, your e-mail software will let you attach a photograph to your message and send it to your aunt.

Adding a digital camera

A digital camera can be a useful peripheral or just a great gadget to play with. Either way, connecting it to your PC means you can view, edit and print your own pictures.

During the past couple of years the digital camera has exploded onto the market, offering the user error-free photography and much, much more. The ability to take a picture, check it on a built-in LCD screen and then either save or retake it, is quite a draw for gadget-loving computer users. Add to that the ability to transfer pictures on to your PC – to include in a document, Web page or email – and they become almost essential buys.

In fact, for the would-be digital photographer, the only potential complication comes in the various different ways that digital cameras connect to the computer. Most

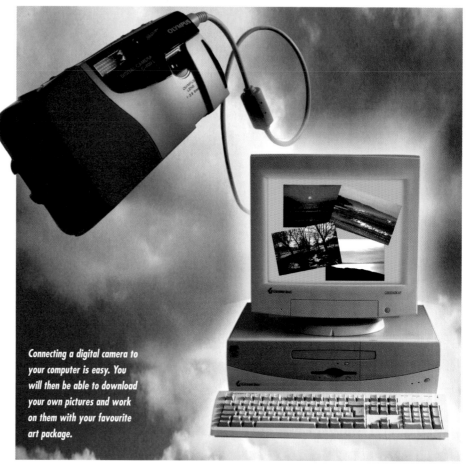

Connecting a digital camera to your computer is easy. You will then be able to download your own pictures and work on them with your favourite art package.

include all the cables and software disks or CD-ROMs that you will need, but you must still check that you can connect it to your computer with the minimal amount of fuss before deciding which one to buy.

● Latest technology

Digital cameras are evolving rapidly, but the most common way of connecting one to a PC is still by means of a serial cable. This is simple, as we show opposite, but relatively slow and it means you might have to switch the computer off before making the connection. The USB connection is becoming increasingly

more common. This type of cable is much faster and you do not need to switch off your PC to make the connection. All modern PCs have USB capability, but with an older one you might have to use the serial connection.

In the exercise opposite, we show how straightforward it is to connect the camera to your computer by using a serial cable. Once this is done, you can use the camera's software to see small thumbnail-sized previews of the photos you have taken and decide which ones to transfer to your computer's hard disk, and which ones you

With a digital camera, an inkjet printer and good quality paper, quite astonishing results can be achieved almost instantly.

don't want to keep. Most cameras also come with photo-editing programs. Depending on the make and model of your camera, you might find that such software varies widely in capability. The simplest cameras allow you to vary the brightness and contrast in your photographs, but others include special effects which make it possible for you to twist and distort the photos in weird and wonderful ways.

It's also important to note that if you simply want to print out your photographs, then you can bypass the connection process and buy a simple photograph printer, such as the HP Photosmart. This allows you to connect your camera directly to the printer and print out high-quality prints of the traditional size.

Connecting a camera to your PC

Taking pictures with a digital camera is one thing – making the connection and downloading them to your computer is another. Here we show you how easy this can be.

THE WAY that you connect your digital camera to a computer will vary from camera to camera. Most cameras use a serial cable. One end has a normal serial socket (like that from an external modem), and the other end has a special socket that fits into the camera. A USB connection is increasingly common, while some digital cameras, mainly those models aimed at users with notebook computers, use a PC Card, and a few have an infra-red transmitter to send the signal. Obviously, the latter is only suitable if your computer is equipped with an infra-red receiver.

In this exercise, we demonstrate how to connect a digital camera and then transfer its images using a serial cable connection.

1 Most digital cameras require both the computer and camera to be switched off before the camera is attached (refer to your digital camera's manual).

2 Locate a spare serial socket on the back of your computer and plug the digital camera's cable into this socket. Tighten the integral screws to secure the plug in place.

3 Open the small plastic flap on the side of the camera to gain access to the sockets. Plug the other end of the cable into the socket on the camera. Make sure you are gentle with the camera, as its small sockets can be delicate.

4 You might be able to plug your camera into the mains electricity (using a special adaptor supplied with it). This is a good idea when you are downloading pictures, as the camera can consume battery power quickly.

THE MOVING IMAGE OPTION

The Moving Image Option is an alternative to digital cameras for capturing photos to transfer to your PC. This comes in the form of digital video cameras – many of which can also capture still photographs. They compare well in price and features, and also provide the additional advantage of a video camera, including, of course, the benefit of sound recording.

5 Cameras come with different programs for transferring photos to the computer. It's easy to preview the photos in the camera and select which ones you want.

Understanding scanners

A scanner is one of the most useful and exciting tools you can add to your computer. It enables you to copy pictures and photographs and incorporate them into your letters and documents.

A scanner works rather like a photocopier but, instead of copying a picture onto another sheet of paper, it copies it onto your computer.

It works by passing a bright light over your original page. The light that is reflected back is picked up by the scanner's sensor. The brighter areas of the picture reflect lots of light and the darker areas reflect less.

The scanner converts the picture into data that your PC can understand and sends it down the cable to your computer. The scanning software running on your computer rebuilds the data into a picture you can see on your screen. You can then save the picture onto your computer's hard disk and incorporate it into other documents on your PC.

● What could I use a scanner for?

Scanners have many uses. You can use them to copy photos, drawings, graphs or pages of text. Once you have scanned in your pictures, you can use software to do all sorts of useful and fun things to them, from changing their brightness and

The C Pen manual scanner is really a mini-digital camera with memory. You pass it over the text to be scanned and transfer it to your PC via an infra-red connection.

contrast to using special effects to make spectacular changes. If you have Internet access, you can send your scanned pictures across the world in seconds via email (see Stage 1, pages 154-156).

● Flatbed scanners

There are several varieties of scanner for the business and professional user, but for the home or small office user the flatbed scanner is the obvious and sensible choice. It is versatile, scans at high quality and is reasonably priced. The flatbed scanner looks and works in much the same way as a small photocopier. You lift the lid, place your original on a sheet of glass and the light sensor moves under the page. The flatbed scanner can also be used to scan books, magazines and mounted photographs.

Once found only in commercial offices, the flatbed scanner has now become a popular piece of kit for many home PC owners.

● Flatbed software

Most flatbed scanners are also supplied with a number of software packages that help you get the most out of the hardware. There is software that makes it easier to use the scanners and provides you with easy access to special effects for use in all kinds of documents.

Flatbed scanners were once so expensive as to be beyond the means of all but the graphics professional. However, in recent years prices have fallen dramatically – to the extent that you can now buy a good flatbed

All-in-one devices like this Hewlett Packard LJ 3100 combine scanner, printer and fax/copier in the same box. You can save a lot of space and minimize wire tangling with such hardware.

for as little as £60 and a superior, high quality one for between £125 and £200.

● All-in-ones

Space is always at a premium in the home or office. A flatbed scanner is relatively small but it still takes up desk space – as do your printer and your fax/copier.

However, if you combine all three devices in one box, you can give yourself some more much-needed elbow room. A wide range of such all-in-one devices are now available from leading manufacturers, such as Hewlett-Packard and Xerox. They cost between £200 and £400 – the quality rising with the price.

OPTICAL CHARACTER RECOGNITION

This is the phrase, often shortened to OCR, given to software that can look at a page of text, 'read' it and convert it into text that you can edit in your word processor. This software can save lots of time-consuming re-typing when text isn't available on disk.

It works by looking at the shape of the letters on the page and trying to match them against shapes it knows. This means that if the document it is reading is of poor quality, the OCR software often can't recognize the letter at all, or it makes a guess. For example, OCR software can easily confuse a slightly blurred 'cl' with a 'd'.

The versatile scanner

You may find that a scanner proves to be the best addition you've ever made to your computer system. Everyone in the family will find a way to use it – here are just a few ideas to get you started.

School essays

Adding an illustration can make a world of difference to all sorts of documents, from school essays to business reports.

New wallpaper

Use your scanner to copy one of your child's drawings and you can use it as your desktop wallpaper – it makes a change from sticking the picture to the fridge!

Newsletters

If you help publish a club newsletter, a parish magazine or fanzine, you can use your scanner to bring it to life. 'Published' photos of a club's events always prove popular.

Personalized greetings cards

Scan family photos and print your own greetings cards; you'll find that a scanner is the ideal partner for a colour ink jet printer.

Digitizing your signature

If you send many faxes direct from your PC, you can scan a copy of your signature and add it to your letters.

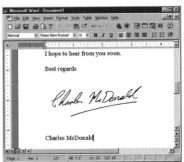

Adding a photo-scanner

A scanner allows you to use photographs and artworks to brighten up and personalize everything from greetings cards and school projects to home-made wine labels and video cassette covers.

Having established on the previous pages what a versatile addition to your PC the photo-scanner is, the next steps are to decide what kind of tasks you want to achieve with it and which type of scanner is best suited to your needs.

There are three basic types of scanner – flatbed, hand-held and feed-through – and each has its own scanning limitations.

The hand-held scanner can scan only small images; feed-through

Scanners come in many shapes and sizes. The EasyPhoto Reader (above) is just big enough to accept standard-sized (12.5x17.5cm) photographs, which can then be retouched, stored, inserted into documents, or emailed from your PC.

models can handle only flat images; and flatbeds are limited by the size of the scanning area. However, there are exceptions. For example, some makes of feed-through scanner can also be used as hand-helds.

● **Port or plug-in?**
Another important consideration may be how the scanner is connected to your PC. There are two types here: scanners that come with a special card that you must install in your computer, and those that simply plug into a socket in the back of your PC – commonly the printer port.

The first type is more popular with business users who do a lot of scanning, as these scanners can transfer the picture to the PC more quickly. However, adding the special card is a complicated task, best left to a computer expert or dealer.

● **Ready to go**
Alternatively, fitting a scanner that connects to an existing port is far easier. This is done in the exercise opposite using a photo-scanner – a special type of feed-through scanner dedicated to scanning snapshot-size photos. Connecting this type is simply a case of removing the printer cable and plugging in the scanner lead. The scanner connector should also have a socket at the other end, into which you can plug your printer.

To install scanner software, follow the on-screen instructions. Once this is done, you can use the software to capture photographs. Software will vary from scanner to scanner – the example opposite will give you an idea of the steps involved. Most kits also include a calibration card, which you scan in after connection to check that your scanner is set properly.

Connecting a photo-scanner

There's no need to open up your computer when fitting most types of scanner. We show you how easy it can be to fit a simple photo-scanner to the printer port.

1 Be sure to turn off your computer before fitting any new hardware. For this project we are fitting a small, simple scanner called the EasyPhoto Reader. It takes up very little space on your desktop and scans your photographs quickly and easily.

2 You will need to locate the printer port. It's easy if there's a printer connected to your PC: simply unplug it and attach the special scanner plug instead. You can then plug your printer into the back of the scanner plug. The EasyPhoto Reader requires its power supply to be plugged into this special plug. Your printer, if fitted, also needs to be turned on after you've connected everything up.

3 Ensure your scanner is securely positioned in a place where you have easy access to it. The pictures being scanned come out of the back of the scanner, so ensure that this area isn't obstructed.

AN ALTERNATIVE TO SCANNING

If you want to import photographs into your PC, but don't want to invest in a scanner, take your prints or undeveloped film to your usual film developer and ask about Photo CD. Some outlets will be able to put your photos on to one of these special CDs. The pictures can then be copied from the CD onto your PC.

Using a scanner

Once you've plugged in the scanner, you need to install the software supplied with it. This will place a new icon on your Desktop, or in the Start/Programs menu. Click on this to start the scanning program.

1 The EasyPhoto Reader keeps all the images you scan in Galleries, so select the Add photo to Gallery option. Then click on EasyPhoto Reader. (Remember, software will vary from model to model.)

2 Your scanner will now start warming up, which should take a few moments. The EasyPhoto Reader shows you how to insert a picture: it should be face up in the Photo Reader.

3 Now you are ready to start the scanner. The EasyPhoto Reader has a green start button: pressing this will start the scan. Some scanners are software controlled, so you will need to click on the on-screen start button.

4 As a photo is scanned, it slowly appears on the screen. When it's complete, you can save it and add it to a library of your pictures. You can, of course, also use CorelDRAW to work on the image (see pages 78-79).

Adding a sub-woofer

Adding a sub-woofer is an easy, five-minute job, with the reward of deeper sound for your music CDs and your games' soundtracks. If you're serious about multimedia, here's how to get more bass.

Although your PC probably came with a pair of speakers, it's unlikely they are particularly powerful or of a high quality. They are, after all, bundled with the PC, and manufacturers give greater consideration to the small amount of desktop space they take up rather than their sound quality.

Standard PC speakers tend to be relatively quiet, tinny and have a poor frequency range. In particular, their small size limits the diameter of the speakers inside: the smaller the size, the poorer the bass response. Consequently, multimedia programs – and particularly games – can sound rather harsh and lifeless.

● Pump up the bass

One solution is to buy newer and better speakers, but although this will certainly help, the central problem remains: speakers with good bass output are too big to sit on your desktop. The best solution is to add a sub-woofer. This is a specially designed amplifier and speaker, which is intended to work with your existing desktop speakers. Some are so simple to install that you have to make no further changes to your system other than finding space for it (see PC Tips, opposite).

You need only connect the sub-woofer to your computer and – without the need for any extra programs (there is no software to install when you add a sub-woofer) – your PC's sound will be transformed.

● One is enough

You need only one sub-woofer, even with stereo desktop speakers. This is because a sub-woofer plays only bass notes; your ear continues to use the sound from the desktop speakers to detect the sound's stereo position.

You can alter how much the sub-woofer affects the sound with simple controls – the on-off switch and, generally, a volume control knob that you turn to adjust the sound level. Don't turn it up too loud, though. Just a small amount of bass makes a lot of difference. Once you have heard this remarkable change in sound, you may never want to switch the sub-woofer off.

BUYING A SUB-WOOFER

All new multimedia PCs come with speakers. Adding a sub-woofer is a simple do-it-yourself matter and will cost around £50. If you don't have a pair of speakers, you can buy a combined speaker and sub-woofer bundle from most computer stores (expect to pay £70 or so). Of course, you should be sure that your computer has a sound card (check in the manual).

If your computer doesn't have a sound card, it's worth getting a dealer to supply and install one, together with speakers and a sub-woofer. Adding a sound card requires opening the computer system unit and is best left to the professionals. The total cost should be around £150, including fitting.

Installing a sub-woofer

Assuming that you already have a pair of speakers attached to your computer, we'll show you how to install a sub-woofer. The exact process may vary with different makes of equipment, particularly the colour and labelling of the cables, so if in doubt, consult the manufacturer's manual.

1 Before you install any new hardware you should make sure your computer is turned off and the power plug taken out at the wall. Remember: your speakers probably have their own power supply to turn off and unplug at the mains point.

2 At the rear of your computer, locate the lead that links your sound card to your speakers. Remove this and replace it with the lead that came with your sub-woofer.

3 Plug the other end of that lead into the input of the sub-woofer. There may also be sockets on the sub-woofer for connecting it to a hi-fi system, but these will be a different size. You will have to plug the sub-woofer, as well as your original speakers, into the mains electricity.

4 Now plug the lead from the sub-woofer into one of the speakers. Remember that, unlike hi-fi speakers, computers generally have one stereo lead going into the first speaker, then out of that speaker to the other, so ensure that this lead is also in place.

5 Your sub-woofer is best placed on the floor (see PC Tips box), under your desk. As you can see below, there isn't much room for anything else when it's on the desk! It will also need plugging into the mains. There is a power switch, usually on the front, which you should turn on. There is also a volume control to adjust.

PC TIPS

The sub-woofer is fairly large, so you probably won't want to put it on your desktop. Most people usually put it under the desk. The only problem with this is that the sub-woofer can make an awful lot of noise and vibration, so be aware of this if there are people on the floor below who could be disturbed.

Making music

Connecting a simple piano-type keyboard to your computer can turn it into a sophisticated music-maker.

Nearly all modern music has been influenced by computers in some way. Musicians such as the Pet Shop Boys and Jean-Michel Jarre have long been using computers to generate almost every type of sound, but even acoustic music has benefited, as computers are used extensively during record production to mix and process music tracks.

Controller keyboards, such as the RolandED PC-180A, don't have any built-in sound synthesizer of their own. Instead, you use them to input notes to your computer, which can then play music through its sound card's synthesizer chip.

However, the most common musical use of computers has been to link them to a piano- or synthesizer-type keyboard. The PC can then be used to store a whole series of notes and play them back later – a technique called sequencing.

● A one-man band

Sequencing means that a single musician can record parts for several different instruments and play them back all at the same time so that it sounds like a whole band. It also means that a would-be musician no longer has to have the manual dexterity to play lots of different instruments. Once the basic notes have been entered, the computer can be used to edit the music (taking out any wrong notes, for example), then play it back fluently and at any speed. This has opened up enormous possibilities for home music-making. With a moderate grasp of the principles, even the inability to carry a tune need no longer be a barrier to having fun with your music-making.

● Computer requirements

Any computer able to run Windows 98 can run music sequencing software. You will, however, need a sound card. Fortunately, all the modern multimedia PCs have a sound card built-in, which will be fine to start with. This has a synthesizer chip, which can be 'played' by sequencing software. You don't even need a music keyboard because you can tell the computer which notes to play using the mouse and it sends the information to the sound card. You hear the music as if there were a tiny – and perfect – musician inside. For creating music, however, this approach is not really practical. A music keyboard lets you input notes more naturally. The computer can also record the key you've hit, how hard you've hit it and for how long. You can then replay this information using any sound available on your sound card, such as a guitar, trumpet or even a barking dog.

Once it's on the computer, you can edit it, perhaps changing the tempo or transposing the melody up an octave. The key to all this is a system called MIDI, which is what makes music on a computer so flexible and efficient. The important thing to

WHAT IT MEANS

MIDI

Standing for Music Instrument Digital Interface, MIDI is really two things: a standard way of connecting one MIDI instrument to another, and a type of computer file that stores the notes of a piece of music.

A MIDI file stores details of which note is being played and its sound characteristics – such as how strongly it is being played. You could think of it, if you wish, as the electronic equivalent of a musical score.

Your computer sound card is a MIDI instrument in its own right. With the correct cable, you can connect it to any other MIDI-compatible instrument.

This top-of-the-range Roland keyboard costs almost £1,000, but it is a professional model with many advanced features.

remember when you play a MIDI file, is that the sound quality depends on the calibre of the synthesizer. If you are unhappy with the sound quality of your MIDI synthesizer you can get your PC to send the MIDI information down a cable to a MIDI music keyboard for a better sound.

● Keyboard types

You can choose from a wide range of keyboards to suit all budgets and aspirations.

Cheapest of the options is the controller keyboard, which doesn't actually make a sound itself – it is the computer that makes the sound. The controller keyboard plugs directly into your computer and allows you to play the notes on the keyboard and

then edit them on the computer screen. When you have finished, you can play the notes through the sound card's synthesizer chip and out of your computer's audio speakers.

A controller keyboard is basically all you need to get started, although you can buy several extra

This mid-priced Yamaha keyboard is programmed with sounds suited to a wide range of music, from classical to pop.

components to increase the sounds available. The next step up is a music keyboard that has synthesized sounds and effects built-in. This type is very popular for home use. However, many low-cost models don't work with MIDI. For computer use, it's essential to have a MIDI keyboard.

You will find a wide variety of MIDI keyboards available from high street stores. When buying, remember to tell the sales assistant that you need a cable to connect it to your computer. Some music keyboards which are designed for home use plug straight into the sound card's joystick port and come with a suitable cable, but many don't come with a cable.

● Built-in sounds

MIDI keyboards differ widely in price, depending on the quality of the sounds inside. The cheapest have a limited range of sounds – more akin to the home organ – and might not sound much better than the synthesizer chip on your sound card.

At the top of the range are professional and semi-professional keyboards. These often have almost unlimited sound possibilities, as you can tweak the built-in settings in many different ways.

You can also buy add-on hardware called MIDI expanders. These devices connect to the PC in just the same way, but they don't have a keyboard of their own. They are mostly used when you simply want to increase the number, or quality, of sounds that you can hear.

MUSIC SOFTWARE

The most important piece of software for the computer musician is a MIDI sequencer. This program is used to record the notes you play on the music keyboard, edit them to correct any mistakes, and then to save the MIDI file on your hard disk. If you're not comfortable with the idea of playing a piano keyboard, most sequencers also let you create music by placing notes on a musical stave on screen.

You also use the MIDI sequencer to play the MIDI files you create, getting it to direct the notes through your sound card's synthesizer chip or out through a MIDI cable to a music keyboard.

You can move and/or copy the notes around at any time, so if you write a song, you need only write the chorus once and then copy and paste it as many times as you need.

The best aspect of a MIDI sequencer is that you can record different parts to build up a piece of music one instrument at a time. For example, you can record a bass part first, and then replay it through the synthesizer, while recording a string section at the same time. What's more, the MIDI sequencer will always play back the music perfectly.

A sequencer screen can look confusing at first. All the on-screen tools act just like the facilities available in a real-life recording studio.

Once you have bought a MIDI keyboard, it takes only a matter of minutes to connect it to your computer. You can then install the software and be ready to make beautiful music.

Connecting a MIDI keyboard

On the previous pages, we have shown how adding a MIDI music keyboard to your computer can open up a new world of sound. However, before you start exploring the joys of creating music on your PC, using music composer programs and sequencing software, the MIDI keyboard and computer must be connected up.

● Types of connection

Some MIDI keyboards are connected to your computer via a cable that is permanently wired into the back of the keyboard itself. More commonly, a special cable (called a MIDI lead) is used. This has a pair of round 5-pin plugs on one end that fit into the music keyboard's MIDI sockets.

The lead from the keyboard plugs into your PC's joystick socket, which is internally connected to the sound card. Once connected to each other, MIDI music information – including which notes you play, how long you hold the keys down and how hard you hit them – is able to pass along the MIDI cable between the sound card and the keyboard.

THE SOFTWARE

The software you choose will play an important part in making sure that your computer and the music keyboard work properly together.

You will need to tell the software – usually a sequencer – that you have a MIDI music keyboard attached. You will almost certainly need some of the information from the music keyboard's manual to set up the software so that it knows how to get the most from your music keyboard.

Connecting the keyboard to your PC is a relatively simple plug-in process, as shown in the step-by-step guide opposite. You then need to install the music software that you intend to use – either a program that came with the keyboard or a separately purchased MIDI sequencer.

● Software set-up

All multimedia computers have a sound card that is suitable for use with a MIDI keyboard. If the sound card has been properly set up under Windows, and is working with other applications, it is ready to work with your music keyboard. However, you will need to set up the computer using the software and instructions supplied with the keyboard.

Once your new keyboard is set up, and with a sequencing program to organize the notes you enter, you'll soon be composing your own music, laying it down instrument by instrument, and then combining it all together using the power of your PC. The only limit is your imagination.

Making the keyboard connections

Thanks to MIDI connectors being standardized, plugging in a music keyboard is simple and takes just moments.

YOUR FIRST step should be to read the instruction manuals that came with the keyboard and sound card (or that part of your computer's manual that covers the sound card). The physical connections (shown below) are quite simple to make – and even easier for those keyboards which have a cable permanently attached, as you can then skip Steps 2 and 3 in the connection sequence.

You will also need to read the instructions for your choice of music sequencing software, making sure it knows where data is being input from. Again, music keyboards specifically made for connection to a computer often come bundled with music software and have more detailed instructions about getting started once the connections are made.

1 Turn everything off before you start. Always adopt a 'safety first' attitude when you add anything to your PC. Make sure everything is properly closed down and switched off before trying to connect any leads. Unplug, to be sure, as this will avoid the risk of damage, not only to yourself but also to your PC.

2 Most MIDI keyboards use a cable that's specifically made to connect the keyboards to PCs (you may have to buy one as it usually isn't included with MIDI keyboards – expect to pay around £20). It has a chunky PC-type plug at one end and a pair of smaller, round plugs on the other.

3 Locate the MIDI sockets on the back of your music keyboard. There will be two or three close together, marked MIDI IN, MIDI OUT and – if there's a third – MIDI THRU. MIDI THRU is used only for connecting extra MIDI devices. IN and OUT refer to signals passing into and out of the keyboard (see box below).

4 Fit the plug marked MIDI IN into the socket marked MIDI OUT, and the MIDI OUT plug into the MIDI IN socket. This might seem confusing, but there's a way of understanding it to make it seem quite simple, see MIDI IN to MIDI OUT box (right).

5 Look at the back of your computer and locate the joystick socket. It will be close to where the speakers connect. The chunky end of the cable plugs into this socket.

If you already have a joystick connected to your computer, remove it. Some MIDI cables have a pass-through socket which allows you to plug the joystick into it. If not, you'll have to swap between the two plugs manually.

MIDI IN TO MIDI OUT

At first glance, the way MIDI cables and sockets connect may seem a little confusing. You connect the MIDI IN plug from the computer's sound card to the MIDI OUT socket on the music keyboard, and vice versa.

It will help to think of the MIDI connections as a flow of musical notes: the notes you play on the music keyboard flow out of its MIDI OUT socket into the MIDI IN plug of the sound card cable and then into the computer. Likewise, when using the computer to 'play' the keyboard with a musical composition program, notes flow from the computer, along the sound card cable and out of its MIDI OUT plug into the keyboard's MIDI IN socket.

Home Learning & Leisure

Flights of fancy

The era of modern aviation began in December 1903 with the Wright Brothers' flight at Kitty Hawk.

Today, flying is commonplace, yet for centuries flight was an unachievable dream. Now you can use your PC to help you find out about the history of aviation and discover how it affects our everyday lives.

Personal service on an early flight

Sir George Cayley

If flight games don't interest you, the Dreams of Flight *CD-ROM might. It captures the romance of the early days of commercial aviation (above, left) and profiles the pioneers of flight (above, right).*

D reams of flying extend back to ancient times and are found in many myths and legends, probably the best known being the ancient Greek tale of Icarus, whose wax wings melted when he flew too close to the sun.

The Dreams of Flight *starting screen provides links to the four main sections of the CD-ROM: Pioneers, Flying Machines, Milestones and Culture. They cover the story of aviation from the Wright Brothers to the technology of the B-2 stealth bomber.*

The earliest statement that flight was a genuine possibility, rather than a dream, is attributed to a 13th century English monk named Roger Bacon. Two hundred years later, the Italian genius Leonardo da Vinci designed a number of flying machines. They never left the drawing board and would never have left the ground, but they did have many sound aerodynamic principles.

Generally acknowledged as the 'father of aviation', Sir George Cayley was an eccentric English engineer and scientist who flirted with flight for 60 years. In 1804, Cayley built a glider with fixed wings and control surfaces on the tail. In 1849, a 10-year-old boy sat in one of Cayley's gliders and flew a short distance when Cayley launched it on his estate.

● The Wright stuff

Controlled heavier-than-air flight was eventually achieved in 1903 by the American Wright Brothers, Orville and Wilbur, at Kitty Hawk, North Carolina, USA. People had finally taken to the skies, albeit to no great height and for no great length of time. However, only six years later, in 1909, the Frenchman Louis Bleriot flew across the English Channel and the dream of flight was fully realized.

● Flight record

There are now computer programs to simulate everything airworthy – from biplane dog-fights to an Atlantic Airbus crossing. But for people interested in the story of aviation, *Dreams of Flight* is a record of the realities that stemmed from the

The most expensive aircraft ever, the $865 million B-2 stealth bomber, was built to evade enemy radar.

dreams of the aviation pioneers and as such has great educational value.

The history of flying is not only a fascinating subject in itself, it is also great to explore in the classroom. It can be used to help bring alive other subjects, ranging from mythology to history and science. Aviation has even been influential in art and design. And *Dreams of Flight* is

packed with information: not just on the scientists, engineers and pioneers, but also the everyday impact that flying has on everything, from fashion through to household items. It explores how aircraft were quickly adopted to transport mail over long distances and how the airmail services in turn helped not only in the development of civil transport aircraft, but also in determining the routes the civil airlines adopted during the 1920s. The colourful presentation will encourage even younger users to dig deeper into the wealth of information, where they will be able to discover facts like the origin of the term 'Jet Set' and exactly how luxurious the early airliners actually were.

● Air power

For people who are enthused by the military uses of aircraft, *The Encyclopedia of Military Aircraft and Aviation: Warplanes* is a comprehensive survey of military aircraft and the conflicts in which they have been engaged between 1976 and 1994. In that period alone, more than 500 types of military aircraft have been in service and they are all described in detail on the CD-ROM.

● Action stations

The wealth of detail extends from the design and purpose of each aircraft, through to its armaments and information about whether or not it is still in service. The details include full dimensions and, with a few exceptions, the aircraft are illustrated. There are more than 1,000 photographs and many are accompanied by live video footage.

After you have looked around the airbases and read about the weapons systems, it is even possible to fly off in one of the aircraft, on screen at least, in the fully functioning simulator program that's included on the CD-ROM.

CONTACT POINTS

Both the *Dreams of Flight* and *The Encyclopedia of Military Aircraft and Aviation: Warplanes* CD-ROMs are available from Focus Multimedia (tel: 01889 570156). Visit the Focus Multimedia Website for details of retailers stocking these titles: www.focusmm.co.uk

The Internet is a great way of finding out more about aircraft from around the world. Even the Red Arrows display team has its own Web site.

To capture the atmosphere of military flight, The Encyclopedia of Military Aircraft: Warplanes' screens resemble the cockpit of a fighter aircraft.

Any history of aviation would be incomplete without reference to the Douglas DC-3, the first of which rolled off the production lines in the 1930s and more than 1,000 of which are still flying today.

SITES TO @ VISIT

The aviation community has always been international and has embraced the opportunities offered by the Internet. Here are just a few of the many places to start learning about aviation on the World Wide Web.

Visit the National Aviation Museum of Canada and see its excellent online exhibits: www.aviation.nmstc.ca

At the home page of the Red Arrows, you'll discover more about the pilots, the planes and the next display dates: www.deltaweb.co.uk/reds/team/

There is also the online DC-3 Aviation Museum: www.centercomp.com/dc3/

If you don't often get the chance to visit the world's best art galleries, you can take advantage of the wonders of computer technology and bring the great masterpieces to you.

Modern art

Appreciation of art can be a time-consuming and expensive pursuit. You may have to travel great distances – invariably to different countries – to view the masterpieces and, when you arrive at the gallery, there are often hefty entrance fees and long queues with which to contend.

Also, many of the world's most famous paintings are protected by glass screens and there is rarely the necessary amount of information accompanying the paintings to satisfy your curiosity about the artists' inspirations and intentions. Fortunately, there's another way to indulge your passion for paintings – have the exhibition brought to you by your computer.

Although viewing the work of a great master on your PC isn't the same as seeing the real picture, there are many advantages, not the least of which is that you can take your time to absorb the many facets of a great work of art.

● Art on CD
The range of CD-ROM titles on the world of art is comprehensive. You'll not only find entries for most

This is the beautifully presented Encyclopedia of Great Artists' *main screen. Moving your mouse cursor over all the objects in this artist's studio will lead you to different areas of the program.*

of the world's great artists on CD-ROM encyclopedias, such as Microsoft's *Encarta* and The Hutchinson *Multimedia Encyclopedia*, but there are also many CD-ROMs dedicated to the appreciation of art. *The Encyclopedia of Great Artists* (Focus Multimedia) provides a fascinating overview of the life and work of many great painters. You can study the artists themselves and chart their lives, work and artistic influences. Or you can study the paintings, many of which are accompanied by expert narration. There is also a timeline which lets you explore art by period and an atlas so that you can see how artistic innovations and developments

happened at various times and in different parts of the world.

It's possible to take a virtual 'stroll' through the Great Artists *CD-ROM, just as you would in a real-life art gallery, stopping to examine in more detail any paintings you like.*

A section called Topics explores many types of painting, such as portraiture, still life and landscape, while Themes delves into the types of subject which have attracted the artist's eye. Material and Methods looks at what tools the artist used and how they were employed to create the effects the artist wanted. In the Workshop, you can learn about art techniques and there is a selection of video documentaries. These explain topics such as what X-rays reveal beneath the surface of a painting and the painstaking restoration work that is undertaken on a painting that has been damaged (such as a Leonardo Da Vinci cartoon which suffered a shotgun blast).

● Art on the Web

If part of the pleasure of paintings is derived from the magnificence of the art galleries in which they hang, there

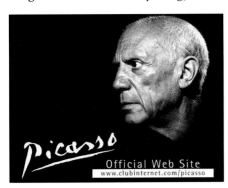

The Picasso Web site at www.clubinternet.com/picasso gives a fascinating online insight into his life and works.

Using the **Great Artists** *CD is like visiting a gallery with your own tour guide. The* **Umbrellas** *by Renoir (right) is seen in a new light when you are shown the different clothing in the picture, which spans changing fashions over the five years the artist spent on the work.*

One of the video documentaries on the Encyclopedia of Great Artists CD-ROM looks at gold leaf restoration.

are several CD-ROMs that will take you on a tour of some of the world's finest. The web offers art lovers an increasingly rich and effortless way of exploring both the world's great collections and the lives and works of individual artists. A starting point for exploring the variety of contemporary art is www.art.net, where you can check out the work of all kinds of artists from all over the world.

The world's great museums and art collections also have a substantial presence on the Web. Britain's Tate Gallery site (www.tate.org.uk) is particularly useful as it gives good coverage of the collections at its sites in St Ives, Liverpool and London. The

Web site for Russia's State Hermitage Museum (www.hermitage.ru) gives a stylish and revealing insight into one of the world's greatest museums. On the other side of the world, the National Gallery of Australia's Web site (www.nga.gov.au) displays a comprehensive collection of all kinds of indigenous art works.

● Looking closer

There are many CD-ROMs dedicated to artists, such as the Renaissance genius Sandro Botticelli (EMME Interactive). This disk explores the motivation, techniques and works of the artist in greater detail than is possible on the broader coverage CDs. There are 200 pictures and an hour of audio commentary to accompany the animated analysis of his work. EMME Interactive has many other artists listed on its French Web site – but an English version is coming soon. It's a near certainty that any artist you can't find on a CD-ROM, you'll probably find on the Internet.

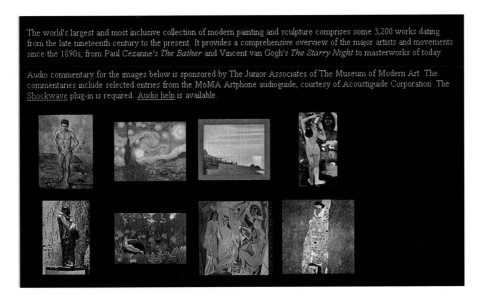

The world's largest and most inclusive collection of modern painting and sculpture comprises some 3,200 works dating from the late nineteenth century to the present. It provides a comprehensive overview of the major artists and movements since the 1890s, from Paul Cézanne's *The Bather* and Vincent van Gogh's *The Starry Night* to masterworks of today.

Audio commentary for the images below is sponsored by The Junior Associates of The Museum of Modern Art. The commentaries include selected entries from the MoMA Artphone audioguide, courtesy of Acoustiguide Corporation. The Shockwave plug-in is required. Audio help is available.

New York's renowned Museum of Modern Art has probably the richest art collection in the world. Its Web site (www.moma.org) is appropriately lavish and detailed.

Designing your home

If you've grown tired of the way your home looks, why not give your rooms a face-lift by changing their layouts? Your computer, as always, can help.

Have you ever spent a day moving all your furniture around to see if the sideboard looks better in that alcove or against the wall? Everything probably ended up back where it started and all you had to show for your efforts were a strained back and aching muscles.

A far better way of rearranging a room is not to move the furniture at all, but to draw a scale plan of the room and position scale drawings of the furniture on it. This way you can try out all the possible arrangements to find the one you like the best.

● No drawing skills required

While it might seem like a great idea, for most of us drawing a scale plan is about as easy as performing brain surgery. This is where your PC can help. There are computer programs that allow you to create scale room plans, letting you see what a room

Once you've got the structure and layout right in Floor Plan 3D, *you can furnish your home and take a virtual walk through to check that it provides you with the effect you want.*

would look like with your furniture in different places. The software will also add different colour schemes. Some programs will even produce a three-dimensional design you can 'walk' through.

● Drawing floor plans

A good CD to start with is *Floor Plan 3D* in the Essentials series from Focus Multimedia. This gives you many of the tools used in professional design, but in a simplified form. You can draw floor plans using the set of easy tools provided or you could take one of the sample plans and modify it to your own taste.

The floor plan shows the outer walls, doors, windows, and the internal dividing walls. To add features you simply select from a drop-down menu, view the options and then

drag and drop the desired element – such as a window or fireplace – into position. For complicated features such as staircases you might have to select dimensions from a dialogue box. To see what your dream home looks like in three dimensions, *Floor*

Floor Plan 3D *lets you take a pre-existing design and modify it – and you can choose to view it in 3D, too.*

Bob Vila's Home Design has handy wizards to help you through the trickier bits, such as this 3D Roof Editor, which helps you design a roof for the building you are planning.

Plan 3D gives you a three-dimensional view that can be modified from a simple dialog box, allowing you to select which layers of the building will be displayed, where the light source comes from, and so on. You can also take a three-dimensional tour through the interior,

There's no shortage of furniture choices in 3D Dream House Designer 2000.

3D Dream House Designer 2000 allows you to view the house as a solid 3D image...

viewing the rooms with their furniture in position. *Floor Plan 3D* is a great way to judge the effects, for example, of demolishing an internal wall. There's no mess or expense and you can rebuild, instantly.

● Designing with Dream House

3D Dream House Designer 2000, from Data Becker, is a larger and more fully-featured program, offering higher levels of control and precision. It comes with a correspondingly hefty manual, which you will need to spend some time with to get the most out of the software but the effort is repaid in the richness of the designs and views you can create. As with *Floor Plan 3D*, you can choose to start from scratch or to use a sample design. Begin with a blank sheet and

...or as a wireframe, so you can see internal structures, such as staircases.

then play around with the samples. The program supplies a handy wizard to get you through the first few steps. You can view your construction as a plan, but in 3D you can see it both in perspective (solid) or in wireframe.

Once you've got a structure and room layout, you need to furnish it. *3D Dream House Designer 2000* scores well on this point; there's a massive range of furnishings to put in the rooms.

● Do-it-yourself home design

Bob Vila's Home Design from Mattel Interactive supplies much the same mix of architecture and design as *Floor Plan 3D* and *3D Dream House Designer 2000*, but it aims to provide a friendlier approach, in the shape of Bob Vila – one of America's 'most popular Do-It-Yourselfers'. A separate module of the CD comprises video sequences of Bob giving you tips on designing and building.

The design software is similar in operation and features to *Floor Plan 3D*. This means it's pretty easy and intuitive to use. It also contains a range of 1001 sample homes. When it comes to dealing with fiddly, but essential, elements (such as a roof) the software is helpful, giving you three separate views on screen.

All three of these programs require quite a bit of effort if they are to be genuinely useful. But that is only to be expected from design software that gives you desktop tools that only a few years ago were, for price reasons alone, available only to professional architects and builders.

CONTACT POINTS

Floor Plan 3D
Focus Multimedia
Tel: 01889 570156
Price: £9.99*

3D Dream House Designer 2000
Data Becker
Tel: 01420 22707
Price: £39.99*

Bob Vila's Home Design
Mattel Interactive
Tel: 01664 481563
Price: £30.00*

*UK prices

At the movies

Lights! Camera! Action! Bring all the adventure and romance of the movies into your home, straight from the silver screen on to your computer screen.

The connection between your PC and the cinema can be traced back to the very first few games that were written for the earliest home computers.

A *Star Trek* game was released even before the first *Star Trek* feature film was made. Based on the TV series, it was one of the first examples of a computer game picking up on popular culture. However, with its tiny '*' character representing the spaceship, it could not look more basic compared with today's CD-ROM multimedia spectaculars.

● Hollywood and video games

After many years of video games based on movies, there are now movies based on video games. Unfortunately, films such as *Super*

Mario Bros, Mortal Kombat 1 & 2 and *Wing Commander* all proved to be pretty poor, although a lot is hoped of the forthcoming *Tomb Raider* movie – featuring a 'real' Lara Croft – and the much-delayed film version of shoot-'em-ups such as *Doom* and *Quake*.

Indiana Jones and the Infernal Machine *marks Dr Jones' fifth outing on the PC, but his first in 3D.*

● The right connections

Your PC has movie connections in more ways than just game playing, though: there are interactive film guides available on CD-ROM; you'll find movie Web sites run by both the film companies and devoted fans; and powerful computers have been used by movie studios to create entire films, with only the voices being provided by real actors and actresses.

● Essential merchandise

When a film has been released, a spin-off game can become a major part of the merchandising throughout the shelf-life of the film. Even if the film had nothing whatsoever to do with computers or the Internet, by the time it is released it will almost certainly have taken up a place in one of the increasing number of PC movie guides.

● Games based on films

The science fiction genre, of course, seems to lend itself to the medium of computer games particularly well, but you will also find other types of film on your PC. After the video game version of *Indiana Jones and the Last Crusade* came a new graphic adventure, *Indiana Jones and the Fate of the Atlantis*, with a completely original plot. The game was so good that it's rumoured to be the basis of the fourth *Indiana Jones* film. Even if that film doesn't get made, there is now a new 3D *Indiana Jones* game on its way as well.

Other film series have struggled to produce games that do them justice. Although several attempts have been made over the years, there has never been a truly satisfying game based on the *Jurassic Park* or *James Bond* films.

HOW MOVIES INFLUENCE GAMES

For every game which is officially licensed from a motion picture there are a dozen that are unofficially 'influenced'. In fact, there is scarcely a science fiction game in existence that hasn't been influenced by classic films such as *Star Wars*, *Alien* and *The Terminator*. Other types of films have also influenced some recent titles. *Resident Evil* seems to owe most of its plot to George Romero's series of zombie movies, and the classic *Driver* game appears to be based on the car chases in the Steve McQueen film *Bullitt*, even down to the San Francisco setting and cars used.

In part this seems to be because some films, no matter how action-orientated they may be, just don't translate well to the PC screen; even the longest of films tends to have only three or four unique action scenes and this just isn't enough to fill even the shallowest of PC games.

The most successful movie-based games are those set within the 'universe' of a film, but which aren't strictly based on the movie's plot. The original *Star Trek* games, which have the freedom to create a plot better suited to a computer game, always tend to be more successful than those trying to translate a two-hour film script into a game with more than 40 hours of gameplay. The *Star Trek* game, *Generations*, is a great example that takes full advantage of your PC's multimedia abilities.

Film itself may be on the way out. Some films – such as Disney's Toy Story – have been made almost entirely on large banks of powerful computers.

May the force be with you!

Use your PC to delve into the amazing world of *Star Wars*.

LUCASARTS RELEASED their behind-the-scenes guide to the world of *Star Wars* just as the hype for the 'prequel' *Episode I – The Phantom Menace* was beginning to build up. *Behind the Magic* is the best example of many similar movie guides, excelling through its superb presentation and attention to detail. Care has been taken to ensure that those with only a passing interest in the films can still find something to amuse them. In fact, the guide has often been described as more fun to use than some games are to play.

Behind the Magic features a plethora of previously unseen material. This includes interviews with cast and crew, video footage of some hilariously bad auditions from the original cast, and a number of scenes cut from the first film that can only be seen as a part of this package.

Characters

This section contains information on a huge range of characters from the *Star Wars* movies, novels and comics. It is split into three sections: Main Characters; Aliens & Creatures; Groups & Organizations. Depending on their prominence within the movies, each entry may have a full biography, image gallery, video and sound clips, behind-the-scenes information and even a trivia question.

Technology

The Technology section looks at the vehicles, weapons and devices of the *Star Wars* universe. Each item has its own screen of information organized in a similar manner to the Character entries, although here each ship has its own rotatable 3D model for you to examine. Highlights of this section include a 3D walking tour of the Millennium Falcon and an interactive 'weapons test'.

Episode 1 preview

This sneak peak at the most recent *Star Wars* movie doesn't reveal much in the way of plot details or images, but is an interesting taster of the movie, with detailed pictures and models and some fascinating interviews.

Scene by scene

Perhaps the most interesting section of the guide includes an annotated scene-by-scene script guide, complete with production notes, images and commentary from George Lucas and many of his crew members.

From film reels to CD-ROM

There have been film licences since the earliest days of video gaming. Here are some of the more recent offerings.

IN THE EARLY DAYS of video games, film licences had a poor reputation. Often the licence was added at a late stage in a title's development, simply to bolster the appeal of an otherwise lacklustre product.

Nowadays games companies are more in tune with the movies, although many titles do still fall into the trap of featuring too many game styles in a vain attempt to simulate every action scene in a film. Over the next two pages we'll look at some classic examples of movie-licensed games. Most of them are successful games in their own right and, rather than being afterthoughts, are produced with help from the original movie crew and actors.

Star Wars: Episode I – The Phantom Menace

As if there weren't enough *Star Wars* games already, George Lucas' own company LucasArts has released a game based on the new 'prequel' – the first of the new trilogy of films. The game is a departure from previous *Star Wars* games in that for the first time it attempts to follow the entire plot of one of the films. Most of the game is played from an innovative quasi-overhead viewpoint. Players can take control of four of the film's main characters: Obi-Wan Kenobi, Qui-Gon Jinn, Queen Amidala and Captain Panaka.

The game's publishers planned for this title to be one of the biggest selling video games ever, thanks to a high-profile simultaneous launch on both the PC and the PlayStation games console.

Blade Runner

Science fiction films and computer games go together like bacon and eggs. But there's a world of difference between the action-based *Star Wars* movies and the more cerebral style of *Blade Runner*. Not a big hit on its original release, the film has since achieved a cult following and is widely regarded as one of the best 'serious' science fiction films ever made. Fittingly, the game is far from being a simple shoot-'em-up, but is instead a dialogue-

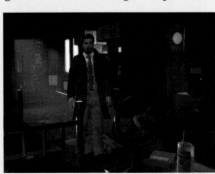

orientated graphic adventure. To ensure that the plot is not predictable, the game's story is different from the film's, although most of the central characters look and act similarly to those that Harrison Ford encountered. Although the game comes across as a watered-down version of the film, it is a brave and rare attempt at an intelligent adult adventure.

Braveheart

Braveheart is a rather unusual film to find being converted to game form, for like the film games of old, the licence to Mel Gibson's epic was only added late in the game's development. Fittingly produced by a Scottish programming team, *Braveheart* is a real-time strategy game that has you controlling the fate of the Scottish nation in an attempt to unite the various clans and defeat the invading English.

The game is split between two basic tasks: fighting various 3D battles across Scotland, and controlling the overall political picture via various overhead maps and status screens.

Trespasser

The two *Jurassic Park* films have yet to spawn a truly successful video game. Although the movies are essentially action films, the most important set pieces usually involve little human interaction with the dinosaurs, which makes a more literal game translation difficult.

The latest gaming attempt, *Trespasser*, is actually a sequel to *The Lost World* and sees your intrepid female character stranded on a dinosaur-filled island.

WarGames

Games don't always have to be based on the latest cinema hit. *WarGames* was a hit film from the 1980s which portrayed the story of a high-school computer hacker breaking into a US nuclear defence computer. The game is a real-time strategy in the style of *Command & Conquer*, albeit with some impressive 3D graphics – a first for the genre. The premise is that you are the hacker trying to win a virtual war game against a computer to prevent it starting a real war.

A Bug's Life Action Game

Disney Interactive's action game, derived from the computer-animated movie *A Bug's Life*, is from the old style of licensed video games. It follows the plot of the film fairly rigidly and the game style is an obvious variant on a popular style of the day – in this case the celebrated *Tomb Raider* series of 3D platform games. Clearly aimed at a younger audience the game is competently put together, but makes little attempt at originality or furthering its particular genre.

Aliens vs. Predator

There has, as yet, been no such movie as *Aliens vs. Predator*. But the idea of these two modern-day movie monsters fighting it out has long ago been explored in a series of well-regarded comic books, from which an unfilmed movie script was derived. However, where cinema fears to tread, video games rush in, and this is only the latest – and by far the most successful – of various attempts to make a game from the concept. *Aliens vs. Predator* is essentially a *Quake*-style 3D shoot-'em-up with the twist that you can take the role of either a monster or a luckless human marine. The game is excellent at portraying all the protagonists.

Top Gun: Hornet's Nest

No matter how old some films are, they are always viewed as ripe subject matter for video games. As with many popular action films, *Top Gun* has appeared in various pixelized forms over the years. The 1995 hit *Top Gun: Fire at Will!* was an imaginative mix of hard-core flight simulator and more arcade-style action, complete with a well-acted storyline featuring some actors from the original film. *Hornet's Nest*, however, is a more dumbed-down approach to the same idea with the emphasis firmly on flight simulation. But it still features James Tolkan as Hondo, and helps to prove that some movies, and their games, never die.

Tracing your family tree

Everyone is interested in where they came from, and who their ancestors were, but tracing your family tree can be a long and complicated process. Your PC can play the perfect research assistant.

Genealogy, the science of tracing your roots, holds a fascination for all of us. Perhaps we all hope to discover that we are really related to royalty! Your computer can help take the hard work out of searching and collating family facts and then present them in a clear form so that you can see how your family has changed over the generations.

A whole range of family tree programs offer the computer-based genealogist a variety of functions and features. Some software offers a suite of programs including graphics and Internet software, whereas others are useful for creating the on-screen equivalent of a family album.

Here we've taken a close look at Mattel Interactive's *Family Tree Maker*. There are others available, too, such as GSP's *Family Tree*.

● Help with your search

A good genealogy program will be both a source of information and a helpful guide to how to find out more. For example, the *Family Tree Maker* includes a huge index of 220 million names!

However, there are drawbacks – only the barest information is provided for each name and the names are all based on American data. This may mean that you need to buy additional CDs; but the idea is good, and the program could prove especially useful if your search leads you across the Atlantic.

Family Tree Maker is certainly useful as an advisor. It has a huge help section that covers such gems of wisdom as how not to misinterpret old date formats, how to write formal letters requesting information and how to get information out of your relatives! It also explains the

Part of the Family Tree Maker is an index card system (below) that lets you enter and collate the details of relatives whose history you have established.

The FamilyFinder Index of 220 million names (above) points you to the appropriate source for seeking out further information.

1891

1917

Keep an on-screen family album; this one is from Family Tree, a GSP program. Create a multimedia history to tell the story of your family throughout the years.

value of the Mormon church, which has compiled the world's largest database of genealogical information.

Collating information

A genealogy program comes into its own once you have a growing mountain of information. It is pointless collecting all this information if it's impossible to make any sense of it; a clear data entry screen is a real boon. *Family Tree Maker* also remembers repeated facts, such as surnames, and fills them in as you type. The result is a simple but efficient way of entering data.

Family Tree Maker uses the family as the base unit, and you enter the basic information for a whole family at once. For example, you type in the name, place and date of birth (and death, if relevant) for a husband and wife on the same page as the names, date of birth and sex for each of their children.

As soon as a page is filled in, index tabs appear on the side of the screen. These link to family screens for the parents of the husband or wife and for each of the children. Don't worry if you have a very big family as the program can cope with up to two million relatives!

Photo albums

One real bonus of using your PC to help collate your family tree is that you can store more than basic facts. It's especially easy and useful to set up a computer scrapbook to store photographs of people at various ages, and much more besides. People's jobs or achievements can personalize the record, as can voice

recordings or scanned documents such as birth and marriage certificates, award and exam certificates, favourite drawings or paintings and written memories. These will preserve the character of your family for generations to come.

Variety of reports

Once the computer is packed with information then the fun really starts. Your PC can create slide shows of family photos and a whole range of printed reports. These include the traditional family tree, kinship reports that show how people are related and calendars that list family birthdays and anniversaries.

Web sites

The Internet has become an increasingly vital link in the chain of genealogy resources. *Family Tree Maker*'s menu bar contains an Online icon that will take you, in the click of a mouse button, to the impressive *Family Tree Maker* Web site (http://www.familytreemaker.com). Here you can search an online database of 470 million names and find a host of other resources to pursue your quarry.

The site has masses of articles giving advice and numerous links to other Web sites with a narrower focus. There's also a link to GenForum, a Web site where you can

For most programs, when you add new information, the software takes care of redrawing the tree. That's the beauty of using your PC to do the work.

leave and/or answer messages 'posted' by other researchers; with nearly two million messages, there's a good chance someone might have the answer to your question.

The Mormons' Family Search site (http://www.familysearch.org) is, in its comprehensiveness, even more impressive. It logs a massive 600 million names which church members have been collecting for decades from all known genealogical records. You simply type in as much information as you have available in the way of names, and the site brings up its results. Note though that the Mormon church has built this database for other reasons; the idea is that present-day members of the church can 'seal' their ancestors – that is, retrospectively baptize them in the Mormon faith.

PC TIPS

To get the most out of your family tree computer program, you will probably want to store family photos along with the information. One way to get these pictures into your computer is to find a local computer bureau, printer or even a local library that offers a scanning service – you give them your pictures and they'll transfer them to disk for you. This may prove expensive, however, if you want to do this often. Another option is to invest in a basic scanner (see pages 104-107). This device scans your photos into your computer as images for you to print and store. You will probably find lots of other uses for it.

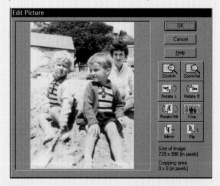

You can just keep a text-based family tree, or you can add photographs to give a fuller picture of your family's life in years gone by.

The Internet

Buying books and CDs from Web sites

Are you having trouble finding that out-of-print book or unstocked CD in your local high street? Broaden your horizons – and chances of success – by shopping on the Internet.

The Amazon.com Web site claims to be the world's biggest bookstore – and with over 2.5 million titles in stock, it's difficult to argue with it. It would be a problem to find a high street shop which is as well stocked. Buying books and other items, such as music and software CDs, via the Internet is really the only way to gain access to an almost limitless amount of choice. Because Internet stores have lower overheads than high street chains, they are also often able to offer their goods at competitive prices.

● Shop until you drop
Buying items from Web sites is very much like buying from a catalogue. As well as the increased range of items on offer, the sites also allow you to use the power of your Web browser and its own search engines to look for specific books or CDs (or any other item you are after). These site-specific search engines enable you to look for books by a particular author, search for books when you know only a portion of the title, or just look for those that cover a specific subject or were published during a certain period.

Most sites organize their wares into useful categories, such as thrillers and non-fiction for books, or modern jazz and heavy metal for music CDs.

Some of the larger sites go even further and offer reviews of their products (often written by members of the public who have bought the item previously), buyer's guides, author/band biographies, links to related fan sites and much more.

Now that e-commerce has really taken off, the breadth and depth of what's on offer has increased. So you won't just find the best-selling books and the top 10 CDs. Instead, you can explore just about any interest you have, from audio books to 16th-century music.

Over the next few pages we describe some of the most popular sites around. But if your own particular interest isn't there, don't despair. Simply use the powers of your favourite search engine (see Stage 2, pages 136-137) to seek it out; the chances are that there will be a choice of sites out there that can deliver the goods.

LANGUAGE BARRIER

Thanks to the Internet, getting hold of foreign books or CDs has never been easier. You'll pay more in postage to have a book sent from France, of course, but the online stores offer such a wealth of stock that you probably won't mind the extra cost. It's easy to find the sites as well. Books On Line, for example, has a drop-down menu giving access to their sites in Europe. Amazon also has sites worldwide.

Books and CDs on the Web

Here's a selection of Internet sites from all over the world, where you can browse through millions of books, videos or CD-ROMs.

BOOKS AND CDS were the goods that kick-started the Web as a way of doing your shopping. Now these sites offer not just a massive range of stock and discounted prices, but, in many cases, extremely sophisticated designs packed with information about the goods on offer. All the sites mentioned here use secure online ordering, and most of them allow you to use an ordinary debit card as well as a credit card. If you can bear to wait for a few days to get your hands on what you want, these sites are a great way to buy both your music and your reading matter.

Online bookselling giants

Amazon – the 'first mover' of online bookselling – has been in business for years. It has now been joined by other excellent sites, developed both by other media giants and innovative specialist organizations.

Amazon

www.amazon.co.uk

Amazon is an online behemoth, with a presence on the Web you can't escape; its adverts seem to be on just about every site you visit. It's one of the biggest e-businesses and worth an absolute fortune. It's not hard to see why investors are excited; Amazon was the first to launch online bookselling, did it very well, and keeps getting better. It has a massive stock of books – around 1.4 million titles – and offers substantial discounts on popular ones, with smaller ones on other books. It also supplies plenty of content, from features and reviews to readers' own comments about their purchases. The site now covers a variety of other areas, including music.

BOL

www.uk.bol.com

Although Amazon had a head start in online bookselling, it doesn't have things all its own way. Books On Line (BOL) is another giant of cybershopping. It's the online outpost of the multimedia company Bertelsmann, which owns the Barnes and Noble bookstores in the US, among many other things. The BOL site offers a database of 1.5 million books, plus many other goodies to make a visit to the site worthwhile. There are plenty of features, including reviews and interviews, and you can create your own visitor profile of tastes so that recommendations will be waiting for you when you revisit the site. In addition, it's all attractively presented.

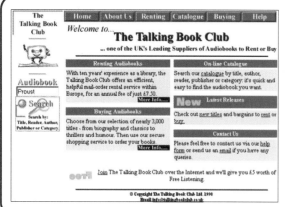

The Talking Book Club

www.talkingbookclub.co.uk

In the modern era you don't even have to read a book to enjoy it: you can listen to it instead, in the shape of an audio book on cassette or audio CD. There's a surprisingly wide range of these, and this site gives you access to around 3,000 titles, covering everything from current best-sellers to unabridged readings of enormous classic novels such as Marcel Proust's *Swann's Way*, which will keep you occupied for a number of days, to say the least. The service provided by The Talking Book Club started out purely as a lending library of such titles, but now you can borrow or buy as you wish.

HMV

www.hmv.co.uk

It didn't take long for the high-street book and music retailers to realize that they needed online outposts. Now all the major chains have some sort of Web presence. In terms of music, the HMV site offers one of the better shopping experiences. It has a comprehensive range of titles, with prices that work out cheaper than the high street, even after you've added postage and packing. It has a neat and attractive layout, while a search for an artist or title brings up not just the thing itself but plenty of background information. Ordering is quick and easy, and they even send you emails to let you know your order is logged and then on its way to you.

Map-guides

www.map-guides.com

If you love to go a-wandering, you'll probably need a map or two to help you find your way. If you want something unusual or particularly detailed, the choices outside large cities are extremely limited. In fact, it's not always easy to get hold of large-scale or rare maps, since these are the sort of thing stocked only by a few specialist bookstores. Because of this, it's extremely handy to have an online store like this one, which keeps a massive stock of maps and guidebooks. If you're off walking or climbing in France, for example, it's good to know that they have the entire range of large-scale maps from the official government mapping agency. The rest of the world is similarly well served. The site also offers a map and book of the month.

Virgin

www.virgin.com

This is the one-stop site for everything in the Virgin empire, from banking and travel to mobile phones and wine. However, as you'd expect from the company with roots in music, there's plenty here to interest the online book and CD junky. Within the site, you'll find music news, reviews, gig guides and charts. There are also pages for many of the bands on the Virgin record label, from where you can view the latest pictures, hear the newest sounds and see up-to-the-minute videos. Bookaholics are equally well catered for with reviews of some 380 Virgin Publishing titles, ranging from biography and sport to new age and crime. Buying online is simple and painfree.

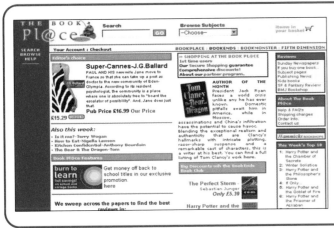

The Book Pl@ce

www.bookplace.co.uk

This British online bookstore has the same range of stock as the multinational giants, but has a number of extras that make it worth a look. For instance, they offer two different magazine-style areas, Bookends (www.bookends.co.uk) and The Book Monster (www.thebookmonster.co.uk), aimed at adults and children respectively. These give more detail on what's happening in the book world and are worth looking at, even if you're not actually thinking of buying a particular book. You can get to the sites either by typing in their Web addresses or via the links on the Book Pl@ce home page.

CDNOW

www.cdnow.com

This is a giant American music store, with European distribution centres, that offers to ship any size of order worldwide. Add what seem to be extremely competitive prices on the CDs themselves, and you need to check this site out before buying elsewhere. In addition, the site is full of useful information, and contains excellent 'beginner's guides' to various genres, such as jazz and classical music. If you can assemble their recommended basic collections, you'll not only be enjoying the music but also, within a short while, be chatting on equal terms with the experts.

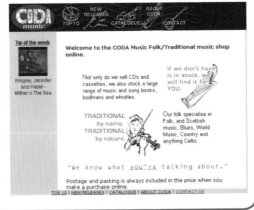

Computer Bookshops

www.ukbookshop.com/compbooks

The online outpost of Europe's largest distributor of computer books and training materials is not exactly a stunningly attractive site. Nevertheless, it's certainly functional, with an easily searchable database, and they'll keep you up to date with new books by email if you want. This site is just the place to look if you want heavyweight computer manuals and related DIY material. And if you've mislaid the manuals that came with either your hardware or your software, the site offers to provide you with what you want so you can get the best from your computer set-up.

Coda

www.codamusic.co.uk

This Scottish online retailer specialises in folk, world and blues music. The site has a pretty large stock, easily searchable by artist or title, and offers to find your desire for you if it doesn't already have it. Post and packaging is included in the quoted prices, so you don't get any nasty surprises when it comes to the virtual checkout. There is no doubt that this is a good resource if the music genres on offer are what turn you on. As well as CDs and cassettes, the site sells music, song books and even traditional musical instruments, such as bodhrans (one-sided drums) and whistles. The site lives up to the statement on its home page: 'Traditional by name, traditional by nature'.

Planning a holiday

One time when you're sure to need plenty of information is when you are planning a trip. So why not use the Internet to discover the wealth of up-to-the-minute travel data and holiday bargains online?

Travel and holiday sites were one of the first categories to make it big on the Internet, for obvious reasons: anyone choosing a holiday – whether a package or a DIY trip – wants as much information as they can get prior to booking it.

However, in the early days of the Internet, finding this information could be something of a hit-and-miss affair, throwing up personal-view snippets from individuals, as well as thoroughly researched and credible sites. There was also little in the way of solid information or online booking facilities from major holiday companies or airlines. But now you can do just about everything on the Internet that used to be done on the telephone or sitting in the travel agent's shop in the high street.

● No-frills flights

The major worldwide airlines have been on the Web for quite some time, offering flight information and online booking. However, these outfits have been premium brands charging premium prices; there hasn't been much going cheap. But a significant development in the late 1990s was the boom in bargain-basement airlines offering no-frills flights at low-cost prices. Even British Airways has had to join in the fun in the shape of its Go subsidiary.

Online booking is an integral part of the strategy of such companies. It's much cheaper for them than using phone operators. And it can be much easier for the consumer, although as these services become more popular, you sometimes find the sites are busy.

● Package tours

Another important development is that while the major package holiday

The world of the Internet has a vast array of holiday information and travel destination choices just waiting for your browser to open. Booking tickets, checking flights and viewing hotels before you arrive are just a few Web facilities.

companies were fairly late to get on the Internet bandwagon, they are now out there in force. Many of them have bold and attractive Web sites, although the quality and depth of the information available varies widely from site to site.

There's a good range of sites, from the cheaper end to the á la carte types – and many sites offer the chance to take advantage of tempting last-minute bargains. However, unless you have a free Internet connection, you'll probably still want to pick up the printed brochures and spend a few hours browsing them.

● DIY travel

Many people prefer to organize their own holidays and the Internet caters for them, too. It can be especially helpful when trying to find somewhere to stay in just about any country. Generally, typing in a search of the town and country you want to visit, together with the word 'accommodation' or 'hotel' presents you with a wide list of possible venues. The sites listed on page 137 contain literally thousands of hotels worldwide, in a range of categories. An increasing number of hotels now also offer online reservations.

Booking a flight online

The Internet shopping revolution now means that you can research and book all kinds of travel – including air travel – online.

HERE WE'LL FIND out about booking a ticket from Liverpool to Amsterdam with the budget airline EasyJet. The procedure shown is broadly similar to booking a ticket on other airlines that offer online booking. These other companies include British Airways, Go (a British Airways subsidiary) and British Midland.

1 Type EasyJet's address (www.easyjet.co.uk) into your Web browser's Address box and press [Enter]. When the EasyJet home page has loaded, click on the important notes link. Read the explanation about how EasyJet's booking system works and read the terms and conditions. When you're ready, you can return to the EasyJet home page.

2 Use the online sales area to specify what you're after. Simply fill in the spaces with the relevant information, either by typing or by selecting from the pull-down menus. When you've completed all areas of the screen, press the 'show prices' button (see inset).

3 Now you're shown the flight information for your chosen location, ranging over a number of days both before and after the dates specified. Click on the radio button next to the flight you want to book (inset) and then click the Next button at the bottom of the screen.

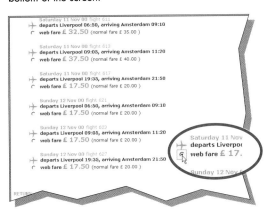

4 The next screen displays the flight you have selected and the price of the ticket. If you are happy with your selection, you then have a choice for going further. At the bottom of the screen is a 'book now' button (inset). Unless you have a very old version of Internet Explorer or Netscape Navigator, click this button to go to the next stage. If this doesn't work, use your browser's Back button to return to this screen and try the other link below it.

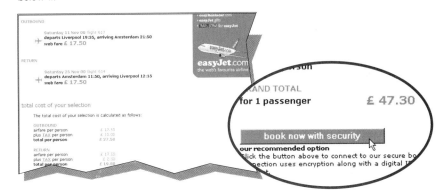

5 On the next screen, all you have to do is fill in the details of the passenger, including your name and address, so that a seat in the correct name can be booked. Scroll down the page to fill in the final details.

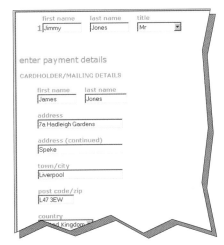

6 Finally, type in your credit or debit card details and tick the box to show that you have understood and agreed to EasyJet's conditions. When you click the 'buy now' button (inset), your card details will be processed and your booking will be confirmed.

Finding out about... Amsterdam

The Internet provides easy access to lots of information about any travel destination. So now you've booked the tickets, here's how you can discover where to go and what to do while you're in Amsterdam.

1 A good place to start is a search engine that categorizes content, such as Yahoo! Go to www.yahoo.co.uk, and start by clicking on the Countries link in the Regional section. Click the Netherlands link when you see a list of countries of the world. Click Travel when the list of sub-categories appears.

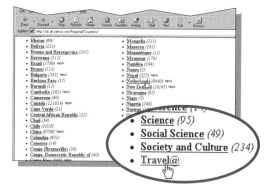

2 Finding a place to stay is a priority, so click on the Accommodation link and then the Hotels link. This page leads to a substantial list of hotels and other places to stay. Read the brief descriptions to see if they're your kind of place. The Hotel Barbacan seems interesting and has a Web site, so click on the link. It offers plenty of information, so you could come back and book, once you've checked out other places on the list.

3 To get a few ideas on what to do while you're in Amsterdam, search Yahoo! for 'Amsterdam', then click on the Local Guides link. TimeOut Amsterdam offers a guide to what's on and where to go. Use your browser's Bookmark or Favorites command and it will remember the page; you can return later by selecting this Bookmark or Favorites again. Now return to Yahoo! to follow some other links.

4 The Internet Guide to Amsterdam is packed with useful information, including annual weather graphs and downloadable maps. The Guide also has a small, but select, section of links to other Amsterdam sites.

5 One of the reasons we're visiting is to see the museums dedicated to Holland's great artists, Rembrandt and Van Gogh. To find out about these, go back to Yahoo! where there are links to sites such as The Rembrandt House Museum (below) and the restored Van Gogh Museum. Both sites give a good view of the respective artists and their work, information on where the museums are and opening times.

6 It might be nice to do a little shopping – particularly for antiques. Yahoo! has lots of sites under their Business and Shopping link. The Antiques and Collectibles category contains a link to the Aronson Gallery, which gives us a good idea of what's on sale.

7 Finally, to check current weather conditions before you go, click the Weather link on the Yahoo! home page, then choose Europe and then type in Amsterdam. You will get a two-to-four-days' forecast – giving you a good idea of what to pack in your suitcase.

Top travel sites

There are plenty of travel-related sites on the Internet, but a few stand out from the crowd for the breadth and depth of what they offer.

Wish You Were Here

www.wishyouwerehere.com

This is the Web site of the popular TV travel show *Wish You Were Here*. Not only are there reviews on all the current locations but an excellent, alphabetical archive lets you roam around the world from Acapulco to Zanzibar. Every destination has a thorough review and an invaluable fact file, providing flying times, currency conversion rates and emergency numbers as well as advice on best buys and places to visit.

Expedia UK

www.expedia.co.uk

This is the UK version of Microsoft's gigantic Expedia travel site. It's huge, so its tentacles reach just about everywhere that a travel site could think to go; the chances are that you can find information here that might only otherwise be found on half a dozen individual sites. Weather, late bookings, flights, maps, hotel directories, car rental, health advice or city guides – you name it, Expedia's got it. And it does it all very well indeed.

Lastminute.com

www.lastminute.com

If you're the type who doesn't plan but does things on the spur of the moment, this could be the site for you. Lastminute.com supplies last-minute bargains, principally in the shape of package holidays and flights, but also more upmarket city breaks (often in posh hotels at competitive prices). Some of the offers are extremely tempting and you can subscribe to a free email newsletter to keep you up to date with what's happening. The site offers easy online booking and is even written and presented with genuine wit.

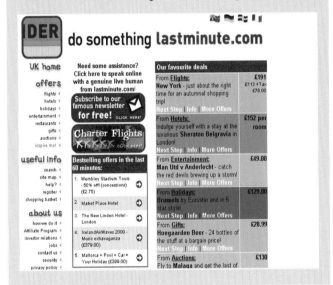

Lonely Planet

www.lonelyplanet.com

Lonely Planet is the big daddy of printed guides for the 'independent traveller'. The Web site offers plenty of good stuff but what makes it vital to anyone thinking of an exotic trip is the Upgrades section, where you find the very latest information on border crossings, visas, safety and so on, that did not make it into the printed version.

O ne thing that the Internet is justly famous for is providing a forum for fans of just about anything. Whether you spend your spare time mulling over the various theories on the TV series *The Prisoner*, or the exact wording of the *Monty Python* parrot sketch, the Internet can guide you in the direction of like-minded people.

For no matter how alone you might feel in your own particular interest, you can guarantee that someone else on the Web feels the same way.

Internet fan clubs

Whether you're a fan of Doctor Who or Doctor Finlay, you're sure to find a Web site to suit your interests. We take a look at Internet fan clubs, from the hugely popular to the downright obscure.

To attract these lost souls, many fans create Web sites for their chosen subject and often start up fan clubs around them.

● Official and unofficial clubs
The term 'fan club' can mean anything from a small group of enthusiasts who keep in contact via email, to an extensive organization (either official or unofficial) with its own magazines (print or email-based) and annual conventions.

Many unofficial fan clubs are free to join, but some charge a nominal fee. Most, though, are non-profit making. However, the same cannot be said of the various official fan clubs you might find.

Although they usually have the more extravagant Web sites, the amount of information and content on official sites can sometimes be less than that offered by more obsessive fans. Of course, this all varies according to the subject of the club and the company behind it.

In the next few pages we look at some of the more reputable official clubs and the more enthusiastic fan sites. As ever, be careful about handing over your hard-earned cash when joining any club. A brief chat with an existing member should soon fill you in on what's what...and, of course, this is incredibly easy thanks to the exhaustive email links that many sites contain.

UNOFFICIAL SITES

You might be wondering how it is that unofficial sites get away with using copyrighted words and pictures. The fact is that often they don't. While copyright holders are often happy to ignore infringements and reap the free publicity, their lawyers sometimes like to flex their muscles and try, usually successfully, to ban various sites.

This happens most frequently with valuable brand names, such as *Star Trek* and *The X Files*, and usually results in torrents of abuse from fans, and a retraction of the copyright holder.

A selection of official and unofficial sites

As you can imagine, there is an almost infinite number of fan sites for just about everything you could possibly think of. Many don't actually advertise themselves as fan clubs, but are still just as effective at bringing mutual admirers together.

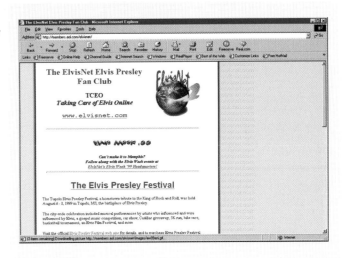

The Prisoner Appreciation Society: Six of One
www.theprisonerappreciationsociety.com

The Prisoner is the grand-daddy of all cult TV shows. The programme, starring the British actor Patrick McGoohan, was unique at the time and, even now, is regarded by many as unsurpassed in terms of ambition and execution.

The series told the story of Number Six (played by McGoohan), a top British secret agent who resigns his job, but is kidnapped and sent to The Village – a surreal town that serves as a prison, and from which he is determined to escape.

This Web site is the focal point for fans around the world to talk about the show and discuss exactly what they think was going on in it.

The surreal nature of most of the episodes has created enough controversy to keep the series alive over the years. Although surfing around the Web site is free, The Prisoner Appreciation Society does encourage you to join the Six of One club. For a fee of £18 you receive a quarterly newsletter and the chance to join the annual anniversary of the show, which usually takes place in the Welsh village of Portmeirion – where the series was filmed.

ElvisNet
members.aol.com/elvisnet

On the Internet, the King is certainly not dead – with a few of the sites even claiming to have been created by the man himself. This is one of the saner sites and tries to concentrate on the facts of his life and music.

Harry Potter Fan Site!
www.angelfire.com/wi/harrypotter

The publishers of J. K. Rowling's best-selling children's books have done Harry proud, creating a fan site

FRIENDS
friends.warnerbros.com/cmp

This is the official site for the hugely popular TV series featuring the young, beautiful but not always very happy (or smart) New Yorkers. It's very well presented and has just about anything a fan could want, including cast biographies, story updates and peeks behind the scenes. There are also well-presented and heavily used message boards and chat areas.

that overflows with content – even if it's not the smartest-looking. News includes details of forthcoming books in the series, together with whatever can be gleaned about the first Harry Potter film. There's a chat area, an online Quidditch game (a sort of trivia affair), and readers are encouraged to contribute their very own Hogwarts stories, which could be displayed on the site.

Sgt. Pepper's Lonely Hearts Club Online
members.aol.com/AMBeatle/club.html

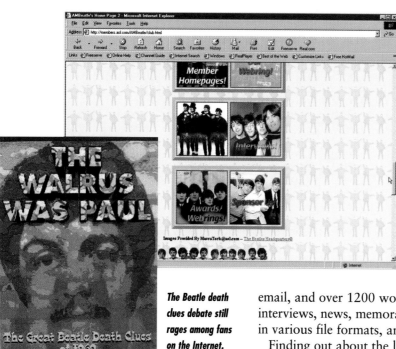

When you are dealing with a worldwide phenomenon such as The Beatles, it's often difficult to know where to start in terms of finding online resources and fans. Sgt. Pepper's Lonely Hearts Club Online, or SPLHCO, as it is also known, professes to be the world's largest online Beatles fan club.

On first visiting this site, this fact isn't particularly believable as the main page is rather amateurish and very slow to download. However, if you dig just below the surface, you'll find a wealth of interesting content. For starters, the club boasts free membership, via email, and over 1200 worldwide members. On the site itself you can find interviews, news, memorabilia, pages created by other fans, the music itself in various file formats, and much, much more besides.

Finding out about the legend that was The Beatles and making new friends in the process has never been so easy, especially as the fan club organizes regular conventions all around the world.

The Beatle death clues debate still rages among fans on the Internet.

The BarryNet
www.barrynet.com

Whatever your musical tastes, you'll find them catered for somewhere. The devotion of Barry Manilow's fans is legendary and they can boast a Web site that is far more professional and attractive than most of its peers. You get a comprehensive biography and discography, complete with pictures and sound clips. There's a lot of emphasis on making pen (or email) pals, as well as taking part in the traditional conventions and, of course, concerts. Tickets can be bought at a reduced rate if you're a member, and there are also various deals on albums and other Barrymania items. If you're one of his fans, you need never feel alone; after all, this site has had over 1,000,000 visitors.

CarryOnLine
www.carryonline.com

This site is a true labour of love that brings together the many fans of the long-running and saucy *Carry On* films. Here you'll find just about everything in the known universe regarding the films, their stars and the memorabilia. There are extremely good biographies of all the regular performers (and the online poll wants you to vote for your favourite guest star), interviews with them from a variety of sources and periods, and detailed pieces on posters, books, videos and all the other spin-off products. In addition, there is a substantial gallery of photographs. One of the best features is a collection of sound clips featuring favourite moments from the films. This site even has its own online mall, where you can buy memorabilia.

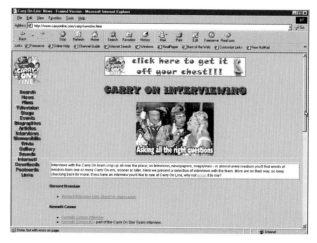

Time Warp – The Official UK Rocky Horror Fan Club
www.timewarp.org.uk

The film and stage show that has the most online fan clubs is *The Rocky Horror Show*. This is the official UK fan club site, but there are many others all over the world. Unlike some fan sites, this one actually goes out of its way to make visitors feel welcome, rather than frightening

them away with obscure lingo and references. In fact, if you haven't been to a live show before, there's a page of dos and don'ts that covers everything from the clothes you

wear to what you're allowed to throw on stage and when. Remember, the average Rocky Horror fan does not favour anoraks, but fishnet stockings – regardless of gender. Despite the potential for lewdness, the whole site is very much tongue-in-cheek, so there's little danger of any children being corrupted by Riff-Raff's devilish ways.

Ricky Martin
www.rickymartin.com

Ricky Martin appeared from nowhere in 1999 to become a world megastar, hence this official site dedicated to the crooner of *Livin' La Vida Loca* and other Latin-flavoured tunes. It's a curiously understated site but there is some

 solid content – a generous stack of Real Audio sound bites from the music and a similar amount of videos. There's also an online shop where you can buy your Ricky products.

MAILING LISTS

One of the most refreshing aspects of fan sites is the genuine, heartfelt input from the fans themselves – an input you can have delivered to your own email address, courtesy of a mailing list. Here's how it works. You send an email to the mailing list address asking to subscribe. Any subsequent mail sent to the list – in much the same way as a message is posted on a newsgroup – will be sent on to you. Similarly, any email you send to the list will be sent on to all the other subscribers. The amount of traffic varies from list to list, but it's not unusual to find yourself getting sent dozens of emails per day for each list you've subscribed to. The level of policing varies from strict to lax, but it is generally commensurate with the subject matter; anyone sending offensive mail could be struck off the list.

Babes and Hunks
www.babesandhunks.com

Forget Hollywood. The film world's new power centre is none other than Bombay – hence the name Bollywood. Films from the Indian subcontinent are becoming increasingly popular with all types of audiences worldwide, and so, too, are their stars. This site, the work of one dedicated fan, is a slick and content-rich guide to dozens of major Bollywood stars. At the core of the site are the pages dedicated to the stars. Here you get good photos, plus a page or so of text, which gives a brief biography of the stars and their latest activities. There are also message boards and chat rooms, free screen savers and wallpaper to download, and all the latest news from the industry. There are also dozens of film clips to view – but you'll need Real Video to view them properly.

PythOnline
www.pythonline.com

One site that is most definitely not sane – and would be a great disappointment if it were – is this official *Monty Python* page. With input from the stars, this is an extremely impressive site for all fans of the surreal and amusing Pythons.

The X Files and the Unexplained

From the bizarre to the disturbing, paranormal phenomena are always hard to pin down. But thanks to the global access offered by the Internet, the answers are out there – somewhere.

An American TV show can't be doing too badly in the popularity stakes when it manages to outdo the turn of the millennium in terms of its influence on the public worldwide. For although the arrival of the year 2000 was undoubtedly behind the surge of interest in the paranormal and the spiritual, it is *The X Files* that focused this fascination and made it fashionable in the build-up and after.

For those few who have managed to avoid the show's charms, its premise is quite simple. A hot-shot FBI agent, Fox Mulder, is in charge of the 'X Files' – a series of unsolved cases which appear to have no logical solution, but in some way involve paranormal phenomena.

Although the FBI tolerates Mulder's passion – which is fuelled by his sister's apparent abduction by aliens when he was young – unidentified factions within the US government (and beyond) are less happy. In order to debunk Mulder's findings, agent Dana Scully, who has a scientific background, is assigned as his partner so that she can report on the validity of his work. The pair then proceed to combat (with varying degrees of

success) government conspiracies, UFOs, aliens, ghosts, demons, serial killers and everything in between.

This might not immediately sound like a ticket to mass-market appeal, but a combination of excellent acting, writing, direction and deadpan black humour – plus a couple of attractive stars – has resulted not only in impressive viewing figures and a generation of X Philes, but also a fistful of awards.

● Made for the Net

Of course, the combination of TV brand loyalty, bizarre subject matter and good-looking actors is perfect for the wacky world of the Internet. This has led to a veritable invasion of *X Files* Web sites, which only adds to the enormous number of 'ordinary' sites dealing with the unexplained.

Some of the latter have obviously been around longer and might cover an almost infinite range of subjects. However, they usually fall into one of three broad groups: the reasonably scientific and organized; the amateurish and illogical – but undoubtedly enthusiastic; and the downright bonkers.

Each category is entertaining in its own way, but you should be careful of the particularly odd sites, as these can be strange to the point of unpleasantness, or

even illegality.

For that reason, it is always best to keep an eye on children when they look at such sites, and to restrict browsing to some of the more responsible sites.

WHAT IT MEANS

X PHILES

Really obsessive TV and movie fans love to give themselves a name that describes their allegiance, the infamous Trekkers and Whovians being perhaps the most familiar.

Continuing this trend, many pun-loving X Files *fans like to refer to themselves as X Philes. So don't be alarmed if you see this term used on any of these Web sites...it's not a spelling error.*

Fox Mulder (far right) investigates the weird and wonderful reports involving anything paranormal, while Dana Scully (near right) applies a more scientific approach, reporting to her bosses on the facts as she sees them.

Exploring the Unexplained on the Internet

**The truth is out there – and the not-so-true as well.
Visit these sites to make up your own mind.**

The Official X Files Web Site
www.fox.com/thexfiles

Supported by the makers of the TV series, the biggest and most impressive section of this site is the guide to each series of the show, split up into all its episodes. Each episode is described in some detail and has an accompanying photo, video clip, audio file and credits list. Other sections of the site give biographies of the actors, information on the making of the show and a forum for fans to exchange views.

Circlemakers
www.circlemakers.org

This is a curious, not to say weird, site for a variety of different reasons. First of all, it's about the crop circle phenomenon – a relatively new area of weirdness that took off in the last two decades of the 20th century. Second, it appears to be put together by a bunch of people whose aim seems to be to debunk the whole thing – which they do by creating their very own elaborate crop circles. On this extremely stylish and witty site, you can see their and others' handiwork, and, as they put it, 'gain some insight into why this tight band of individuals spend their summers out in the fields of England flattening cereal crops in various intricate patterns'. There's plenty of 'evidence' in the form of photos and real audio files. It's a very odd site, but well worth a look.

GAWS
gaws.ao.net

Few fans of the *X-Files*, or X Philes (see opposite) can claim that their enthusiasm for the show is restricted to an academic interest in the subject matter, or an admiration of the cinematography. For although not everyone will agree on whether the two main actors rate as classical beauties, they have both managed to become international sex symbols. There are many sites dedicated to David Duchovny and Gillian Anderson, although not usually to both of them at the same time. GAWS stands for Gillian Anderson Web Site, and is one of the main ports of call for the Scully-obsessed. Here you'll find everything you could wish to know about the red-haired actress.

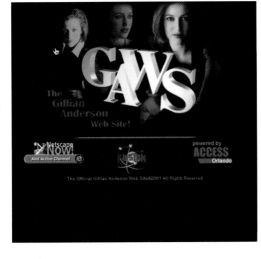

Fortean Times
www.forteantimes.com

Charles Fort was an American-born intellectual who wrote books about science and the unexplained during the 1930s. Fort observed that much research was anything but scientific, noting that inconvenient data was often suppressed or avoided. He thus became convinced that there was much in the world that could not be explained by traditional science, and he sought to document it in a magazine called *Fortean Times*. This has become widely read and the related Web site features some of its stories and pictures. The site has a good links page and an online form for reporting weird sightings and stories.

Anomalist
www.anomalist.com

The Anomalist is another Web-based version of a printed magazine, which is not dissimilar to *Fortean Times*. The publication certainly shares the same admiration for Charles Fort and his musings, but the Anomalist Web site distinguishes itself from that of Fortean Times by having a smaller number of longer articles. These cover topics from UFO sightings to bigfoots. Every story is taken seriously, even though it might be related with a large degree of knowing humour. For the Anomalist site, the truth behind a hoaxed paranormal event is just as interesting as vague facts about a 'real' sighting, since both kinds end up revealing more about human nature than they ever do about how many humps Nessie really has.

The Parascope
www.parascope.com

This site is, in many ways, the American equivalent to something like the British Fortean Times or Anomalist Web sites. However, it's a little more down-market and, more worryingly, is all too eager to believe the most ludicrous of paranormal theories. In truth, there is little actual attempt to explain or theorize on any of the stories reported, but it's quite clear that the writers tend more towards the conspiratorial view of things than accepting the innocent explanation. But this hardly seems to matter as the site doesn't really expect anyone to come here looking for rigorous scientific debate, rather for an amusing or spooky story.

CSETI
www.cseti.com

CSETI is short for the Centre for the Study of Extraterrestrial Intelligence, which all sounds terribly official and governmental, but it's not. It's an organization founded and run by a US medical doctor, Steven Greer, who says CSETI is 'the only worldwide organization dedicated to establishing peaceful and sustainable relations with extra-terrestrial lifeforms'. There's material on Greer himself ('widely regarded as the world's leading authority on the subject of extra-terrestrial intelligence'), field reports of 'sightings', information on where to spot satellites and details of the RMIT – the Rapid Mobilization Investigative Team.

BUFORA On-Line
www.bufora.org.uk

UFO investigation groups are constantly trying to maintain a professional and competent appearance. The British Unidentified Flying Object Research Association (BUFORA) is the UK's biggest such organization and is closely affiliated to similar groups in the USA and around the world. Its Web site is large and well worth a visit. It is split into several main areas: a News section, featuring UFO case studies, opinions and breaking news; a Research section, where sightings are reported and similar observations can be studied; an Investigations section, where current UFO-seeking is documented; and a Members Only section.

SITES TO @ VISIT

There is certainly no shortage of unexplained sites on the Web, so here's a selection from the best of the rest:

News of the Weird
www.newsoftheweird.com
Chuck Shepard's News of the Weird is a collection of strange news clippings from around the world. There's no attempt at verification or explanation; you're meant to read and be amused by the things culled from the small print of every paper under the sun.

Weird Science
www.eskimo.com/~billb/weird.html
Not so much a site in itself as an extensive collection of articles and links to other sites, all of which attempt to put some wonder back into science. There's stuff on 'scientists' transcended experiences' and well-known but little understood phenomena, such as Tesla coils and ball lightning. Following just a few of the links in the site's long list could shake the convictions of even the most hardened of sceptics.

Weird History 101
www.thegrid.net/fern.canyon/weird/history.htm
This amusing little site is really a teaser to get you to buy the book of the same name. You get lots of snippets of wild and wacky facts of history, and a sample from the book recounting some of the more bizarre acts, habits and sayings of American presidents, one of whom – perhaps talking of the paranormal – apparently said, 'I have opinions of my own – strong opinions – but I don't always agree with them.'

The Science Behind the *X Files* HYPERLINK
huah.net/scixf
This is a fascinating site, the author of which has a scientific background. It attempts to cover each episode of the TV programme, commenting on all the scientific and paranormal events featured, complete with possible solutions. What makes this process interesting is that each comment is backed up with a hyperlink to a relevant Web site, allowing you to research for yourself.

Conspire.com
www.conspire.com
On the surface, it doesn't really seem that conspiracies – whether committed by big business or the government – have much to do with the world of the

unexplained or paranormal. But *The X Files* forged a link, so the paranoid world of conspiracies has become synonymous with that of ghosts, ghoulies and aliens.

Conspiracy theories can often be depressing and disagreeable, so it's rather refreshing to come across this site, which takes the whole thing with a pinch of salt. Conspire.com comprises separate sections labelled UFOlogy, JFKology, and Rant, which, as well as being informative, together manage to put the fun back into apocalyptic global conspiracies.

Cryptozoology!
www.ncf.carleton.ca/~bz050/HomePage.cryptoz.html
The term 'cryptozoology' was coined in 1959 to describe the search for (and research into) previously unknown animals. To many this might just imply treks in search of the Yeti or Loch Ness Monster, but, in fact, it has a much more mainstream application in identifying new species of insects, birds and mammals.

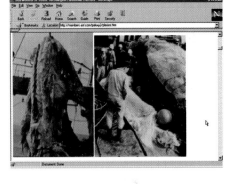

Of course, many people involved in this sort of research still dream of dissecting Nessie or caging Bigfoot, but no doubt prefer to keep this side of things quiet when talking to more conventional scientists.

This site is therefore a mixture of descriptions and pictures of everything from a new kind of beetle with strange joints in its leg, to an amazing picture of what might or might not turn out to be the Abominable Snowman.

Recent sightings of 'large black cats' in remote parts of Britain have excited cryptozoologists and the site has an extensive section on these.

Obiwan's UFO-free Paranormal Page
www.ghosts.org
This site concerns what used to be the major focus of paranormal research: ghosts and the supernatural. The graphics aren't as good as some Web sites, but there is an impressive range of content. Most amusing is the list of haunted hotels, complete with booking rates and tourist information.

There's also a large database of supposedly true ghost stories, sent in by visitors to the site. To top things off there's a huge page with links to ghost investigators, case studies and just about anything else that goes bump in the night.

All creatures great and small

If you or anyone in your family has an interest in natural history, let the Internet bring that interest to life, as it's a rich source of knowledge about everything in the natural world.

Natural history is a huge topic covering the origins, evolution and ecology of the Earth and the plants and creatures living on it. As such, it cuts across many more specific areas, making it somewhat difficult to find all the information you require in a single book or encyclopedia.

However, the Web offers a vast range of natural history sites, so PC users of all ages can explore their interests in many exciting ways.

● Going batty

For example, if you've just watched a wildlife programme about bats on television and want to know more, you can instantly find information from a 'bats' site on the Internet. School assignments will be enriched by Internet research, with many of the best natural history sites on the Web belonging to great institutions, such as London's Natural History Museum, which prides itself on the educational content and interactivity of its sites.

Quite often there will be a list of FAQs (frequently asked questions) on a given topic and they may well provide just the information you're looking for. You can download text to add quotations to an essay or project or even save pictures from a Web site to use in your work.

Of course, the interest in natural history sites is not limited purely to those doing schoolwork. The living world fascinates and astonishes all of us, and the Web is the ideal place to follow up even an idle interest in something you've seen on TV or read about in the newspaper.

● Practical pet help

There's even a practical value too, at the level of caring for pets and other animals. This is particularly true of the rarer or more unusual domestic pets. If your taste runs to snakes, for example, you'll find literally dozens of richly informative sites on reptiles, offering expert advice on buying, rearing and breeding serpents.

It's a fascinating world and such a large one that we can only scrape the surface here to point out some of the best sites around. However, you can be sure that whatever your interest, from fish or fowl to beast, you will find not just a couple, but many sites to inform and entertain you.

It's a jungle out there

As the Internet embraces the latest computer technology, the amount of information available about the natural world may prove surprising.

THE SITES we've selected over the next few pages offer a broad example of the range of what can be found on the Web, from the great institutions of the world to small groups of enthusiasts. What they all have in common is that you'll be entertained as well as informed if you visit them.

The major museums featured all have an 'online gallery' of one kind or another – whether it's a guided virtual tour of the permanent collection or a special exhibition on a specific topic. Some of these museum sites also have excellent interactive and collaborative learning sections, where schools and individuals can contribute to ongoing projects with help from the museum's experts.

We've also looked for sites that will have a special attraction for smaller children – ones that introduce an element of play into learning.

Naturally, we've picked out a number of sites that deal especially well with dinosaurs – an enduringly popular subject with both children and adults.

Florida Museum of Natural History

www.flmnh.ufl.edu

This site is notable mainly for its Fossil Horse virtual museum, which lets you learn about palaeontology and evolution by exploring the fossil record of horses. Clicking on the horse skulls tells you about the creatures, while clicking on the different geological eras tells you about the ecology of the period.

This virtual museum allows you to uncover the fascinating history of the fossilized horse.

The Giant Squid

seawifs.gsfc.nasa.gov

A minority interest, perhaps, but the giant squid is the world's largest invertebrate – and a pretty elusive creature to boot. This online version of a special exhibition at the American Smithsonian National Museum of Natural History succeeds in its aim of displaying the mystery, beauty and complexity of these mysterious, gigantic creatures.

Discover the mysterious squid – how has such a seemingly fragile creature survived so well?

The Natural History Museum, London

www.nhm.ac.uk

This is a site that does justice to a fine collection. There's a great 3D-surround video tour of the Earth and Life galleries, enabling you to take a 360-degree look at the giant dinosaur skeletons. There are even virtual reality fossils, such as this trilobite (below) to look at. To get the best out of this site, you may need to download plug-ins (see Stage 2,

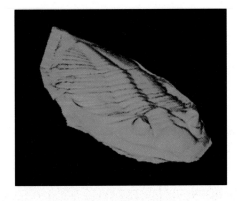

pages 146-147). There's also a Science Casebook section where you can post queries or initiate discussions relating to the areas covered. You might find a discussion of whether dinosaurs really could be recreated from DNA, or even a discussion on whether or not the Beast of Bodmin Moor actually exists, or indeed ever did.

Seaworld

www.seaworld.org

This is the site of the aquatic theme parks of the same name, with outposts in both Florida and California.

At the Seaworld site, you can journey to Florida and visit the wonderful aquarium.

It's bright, breezy and commercial, but nevertheless contains lots of educational resources. Choose the aquatic safari option and you'll be able to discover a wealth of information about fish. And, by viewing the animal enclosures with the Webcam, you can check out what's happening as it happens.

Chicago is home to one of the finest aquaria. The Shedd Aquarium houses fish, reptiles, birds and mammals.

Shedd Aquarium

www.sheddnet.org

This Chicago aquarium is one of the biggest and best-stocked in the world. The colourful site contains lots of entertaining information about the aquarium itself and is also packed with fascinating information about the creatures of the deep. Fact sheets give you an informative picture of the exhibits and provide you with data – all of which make a visit to this site rewarding.

Smithsonian Institution National Museum of Natural History

www.mnh.si.edu

The leading natural history institution in the USA has an excellent presence on the Web. You can find out all you need to know about the museum and examine a number of well-presented and informative online exhibits. The virtual tour of the museum is easy and you won't find it hard to get to the dinosaurs. There's a section on global warming and an innovative exhibit called the Hologlobe, which shows the world from an astronaut's viewpoint to demonstrate various ecological and climatic points.

See Earth as the Galileo spacecraft saw it – looking back on its journey to Jupiter. The Smithsonian's Hologlobe (left) lets you do this.

The Smithsonian Institution has a section called Portraits of Smithsonian Science (right), which brings to the fore some of the personalities who usually remain behind the scenes.

Sites for children

There are special sites to encourage younger children to learn about animals over the Internet.

Bats4Kids

members.aol.com/bats4kids

This is a site that aims to take the terror out of bats! Designed clearly for children, this site removes the mystery of these nocturnal creatures by presenting true and fascinating facts about them. For example: Where do bats live? Why aren't they birds? What are the myths about bats? All the answers are here, in a colourful and clear site. You can play a game of bat concentration (a simple memory game) or you can enter the bat quiz – or even visit a bat cave. Children will love this site, but adults may also learn much of interest.

Bats may be frightening for some children, but this site quickly explodes the myths, revealing much about these fascinating creatures.

The bat cave provides a bat puzzle, bat crossword and a bat word search game to test young visitors on how much they can remember.

Walking with Dinosaurs

www.bbc.co.uk/dinosaurs

The TV series that outdid *Jurassic Park* in its recreation of dinosaurs has a lavish site, rich in resources. Here you'll find information on the creatures and their habitats.

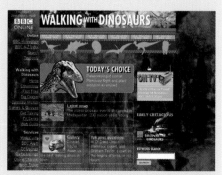

St. Louis Science Center

www.slsc.org

This site contains an Ecology and Environment Past online gallery, which is sub-divided into several sections, including Geological Timeline, Fossils and Do or Die. The Geological Timeline is of most interest, giving a guided tour of living beings since the dawn of time. Dinosaurs obviously feature, with colourful dioramas, but so do plenty of other creatures, down to the tiny shrew of 200 million years ago. As well as the natural-history content, the site contains a rich vein of other interesting scientific material.

At the St. Louis Science Center site there are 300 pages of photographs, video footage, drawings and informative text – and that's just in the Ecology and Environment Past section.

When dinosaurs ruled the earth

Dinosaurs provide endless fascination for both young and old alike, so step back in time by several million years and search for them on the Web.

The Field Museum of Natural History

www.fmnh.org

This great Chicago museum has a marvellous collection of just about everything, and good virtual tour facilities. You can take several virtual dinosaur tours, each one of which is informative, richly illustrated (below) and easily accessible to children of all ages. There are games and quizzes, and you can even download a simulated running triceratops. The Field is worth visiting regularly as it's recently bought Sue – the largest and best-preserved *T Rex* remains in existence – so you can follow the preservation process.

UCMP Web

www.ucmp.berkeley.edu

A Geological Time Machine is the highlight of this site from the University of California at Berkeley. It takes you through millions of years of history, discussing the ecology and the creatures that lived in various eras – including the dinosaurs. The site is rich in links to related information and is well illustrated.

The UCMP Website is a vast source of knowledge about fossils, such as this trilobite.

National Geographic

www.nationalgeographic.com/dinoeggs

This 'online egg hunt' is developed from a National Geographic-sponsored expedition and the subsequent magazine article. Researchers 'hatch' fossilized dinosaur embryos and you can then follow their progress. Although this is not an extensive or in-depth site on dinosaurs, what it does it does well, and there are good links to other dinosaur sites. And, of course, anyone keen on natural history is likely to be interested in much of the content of National Geographic.

The National Geographic site is of the same high quality as the respected magazine. Discover the dinosaur egg hunt (right) that featured in a 1996 issue of the magazine and get a behind-the-scenes view, unique to the Internet user.

Internet chat

Internet chat systems offer the opportunity to communicate live online with other computer users all round the world.

Q. 'I've lived in London for four years since I left college. How about you?'

A. 'I start college in Paris next year, it will be the first time I have left Bangkok'

Sending messages to people all over the world via email has long been, and is still, the main reason why people use the Internet. But email does not happen in 'real time': it's more like sending a letter than making a phone call. But it's actually very easy to talk, or 'chat', to other people on the Internet in real time, and not just to a single person, but to a host of participants all over the world. In fact, Internet chat is so easy that it has become one of the fastest growing areas of use.

In the earlier days of the Internet, real-time chat was an extremely complicated business; you had to download substantial programs which could be confusing to use. And finding the 'chat rooms' where people gather was no easy business. Nowadays, the whole thing has become much simpler, largely because the software that powers the chat system downloads in a matter of

seconds. That, together with the massive and growing number of people online, means that Internet chat has never been easier. Just log on to the home page of any major ISP (Internet Service Provider) and you'll find a link taking you directly to chat areas. We show how, and what is available, over the next three pages.

● **People and topics**
Chat rooms cover every conceivable interest. There are rooms dedicated to dealing on the stock market, to soaps, to football and to pop music, to name but a few. There are also many rooms created specifically for certain age groups, such as teens, 40-somethings and so on. And, of course, there are many rooms – with names such as Love Shack, Singles Bar and the like – where the chat often takes the form of more flirtatious conversation.

Whatever the room or the ISP, the format is very similar and easy to use. The screen generally presents a main

window showing the participants' contributions. A narrow window at the bottom is where you type your own, before clicking on Send or hitting [Enter] to send it to the chat room. On the right you will nearly always find a list of the users currently active: in many services you can click on these to get personal details (if supplied) and to send mail to or chat one-to-one with other users, away from the main chat room.

A WORD OF WARNING

Although some chat rooms – such as those on AOL – are monitored by a guardian, the general rule is that they are a free forum. People can, and do, say just about anything, sometimes in very salty language. So you need to exercise caution about which chat rooms you, and especially your children, enter. Fortunately, potentially unsavoury ones are nearly always easily identifiable by their names.

Using Yahoo! Chat

Yahoo! is one of the Internet's most popular sites. It offers a range of services, including numerous different chat rooms which are easy to access and use.

1 Go to the Yahoo! UK site (www.yahoo.co.uk) and click on the Chat link near the top of the page.

2 As a first-time visitor, you'll have to register in order to get a user ID and a password. Remember that you don't need to use your real name – and it's probably advisable to use a pseudonym if you value your anonymity. Just type in your chosen ID and password in the boxes at the top of the page. You'll also be asked to provide some personal details so that Yahoo! can help out should you forget your details.

3 Once that's done, you are taken to the home page of the Chat area where you'll see links to some featured rooms organized by topic, such as sport, stocks and shares, movies and so on. Simply click on the one you want to go there.

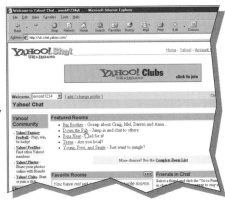

4 Before you can actually enter the chat room, you may have to install the Yahoo! Chat software. This is a Java program that downloads almost instantly; all you need to do is click the Yes button.

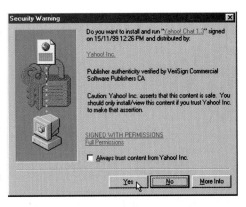

5 Now you're ready to chat. The main screen window shows who is entering and who is leaving the room, and the sender and text of any messages. To join in, all you do is type your contribution in the narrow Chat: box at the bottom of the screen and click the Send button. On the right is the Chatters window showing a full list of those in the Chat room.

CHAT TOPICS

The front page of the Yahoo! Chat area offers half a dozen featured rooms that you can jump straight in to. If you're new to Chat then it's probably a good idea to check these out first. But these are far from being your only choices. The UK version of Yahoo! Chat offers well over 200 categories of chat room, covering just about everything from business and computing to romance and religion. And there are dozens of rooms dedicated to local chatting, so you can check out folk from your very own area.

The vast majority of these rooms are safe and welcoming places, where people go to interact with others and benefit from their advice and experience. The one category you should be wary of, particularly if children or teenagers are going to be online, is romance. There is a wide variety of chat rooms within this category, and generally they are pretty safe. But rogue chatters can and do make appearances, sometimes with pretty offensive material. Enter these rooms at your own risk, and monitor them carefully if your children are going to use them.

Chatting on AOL

If you are a member of AOL (see Stage 1, pages 146-149), you'll probably find a topic to talk about in one of its chat rooms.

1 Getting into the chat areas on AOL is extremely straightforward. Once you've logged on, just click the Chat channel on the left of the AOL Today screen.

2 The AOL Chat page appears. From here you have a variety of options. Click on the Chat Rooms button at the top to go to a list of what's available.

3 You can now scroll through a list of categories covering a wide range of topics, from the practical to the frivolous. Simply double-click on one to enter the room.

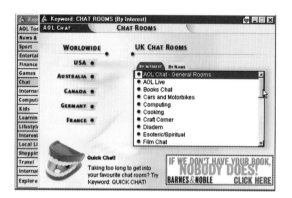

4 Here, by clicking on the heart-shaped link from the first page (see Step 2), we've entered the Love Shack room. This is a light-hearted romance chat room, which is generally very busy and usually has fairly innocuous content. The list of members in the room is displayed on the left of the screen. To join in, just type in your message in the box at the bottom and click Send or hit the [Enter] key.

5 Because AOL is a worldwide service, chat rooms are not limited to the UK. From the Chat Rooms page (see Step 3), just click on the area that interests you – Worldwide, USA, Australia, Canada, Germany, France – and you could be chattering away in a foreign language in no time.

6 AOL also gives you the opportunity to participate in live celebrity chat sessions. From the AOL Chat page (see Step 2), click on the AOL Live link, which will take you to the AOL Live channel. Here you can see what's happening in any given week and then log in at the relevant time.

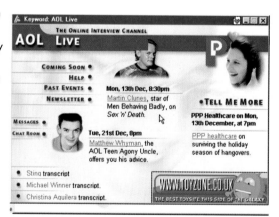

CHAT-ROOM SHORTHAND

New chatters will find plenty of shorthand is used in chat rooms on the Web. One of the most frequently used abbreviations is 'lol', which is a little bemusing at first. It means 'laugh out loud' and is added to the end of your comment if you mean it as an ironic joke, as in: 'Yes, my other car is a Ferrari lol'. Another popular one is 'ROTFL' – rolling on the floor laughing – used only when you find the comment extremely unfunny.

Freeserve Chat

Freeserve's chat rooms reflect the interests of its more than 2 million members – and you can even chat in 3D worlds.

FREESERVE HAS BECOME much more than a simple ISP connecting people to the Internet (see Stage 1, pages 142-145). Its wide range of services mean that it is more of a 'portal' offering a one-stop way of satisfying the need of its users for news, entertainment, listings and Web searching. As such, online chat is an integral part of the offering and one that Freeserve has tried to make as simple to use as possible.

1 To sample Freeserve Chat, go to its chat page (www.freeserve.com/chat/). A list of 20 or so available rooms is shown, covering topics from business to games, and there are plenty of general chat rooms for different age groups. Click on one of them to get going.

2 If you're new, then you will have to download the chat client – the software that enables the whole business. This is a small program that will download in less than a couple of minutes. Fill in a user name of your choice (see Step 2, page 151), select the Java client button and then click the Enter icon (inset).

3 You are taken to the room of your choice. As with Yahoo! Chat, to have your say you simply type in the message in the box at the bottom of the screen and click Send or press [Enter]. Users' comments appear in the main panel. In the right-hand panel, click the relevant tab to select whether to display the users, other chat rooms or the ready-made images that the system allows you to insert in your messages.

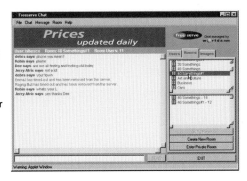

4 The Images panel is very handy. It supplies a wide range of pictures which are shorthand for various moods or comments. Just double-click on the image and it will appear in the entry bar. Then press Send for it to appear in the main window. As we see here (inset), bibesco is not feeling too happy.

5 In addition to these conventional chat rooms, Freeserve also gives you the opportunity to spice things up by entering a 3D Chat world, where you can create one or more on-screen characters (known as 'avatars') and move through a graphic world, chatting with the other characters. To enter this realm, you will have to download a larger program and to register. Go back to the first chat page (see Step 1) to discover details of the service and the link to download the software. The software takes around 20-30 minutes to download. Save it to a location on your hard disk and then double-click the programme icon to install the software, following the on-screen instructions. In order to register, you will have to give your correct email address. Shortly afterwards, you will receive an email notifying you of the code word you must use to access the 3D Chat world.

6 Once inside the world, you take the form of an on-screen shape and you can move around in every direction using the cursor keys. You can talk to others present by typing in your message in the bar at the bottom of the screen. Participants appear as their chosen on-screen figure, with a label identifying them.

7 If you want to change your appearance to that of a person, just click on the AvatarGallery link and you'll be taken to a room where you will find a dozen or so 'types' from which you can choose.

Creating your own Web site

One of the great pleasures of the Internet comes from creating your very own site and having people access it. To actually produce your own Web site is nowhere near as difficult as you might imagine – and we'll show you how.

If you have an account with one of the well-established ISPs, then you almost certainly have some free Web space as part of your package deal. By taking advantage of this space, you have the ability to create your own Web site for other Internet users to see.

You could use this space to set up a site for your hobbies, a site to advertise your business if you're self-employed or even a site that simply says 'Hello world' and contains details about you and your life.

Most ISPs provide at least 5MB of space free of charge. Additional space is available at extra cost, but 5MB should give you plenty of scope to make an interesting site.

● It's just another document

Just like the documents you create in Word or Excel, the pages you make for a Web site take up disk space. Similarly, when you create the pages, you store them on your computer's hard disk. The difference is that to make the Web pages visible to all Internet users, you copy (or upload) them to your ISP.

Your ISP has powerful computers, called Web servers, which are dedicated to storing hundreds or even thousands of Web pages for its customers. Anytime someone wants to see your Web site, your Web pages are retrieved from the server.

● An address for your site

Once your Web pages are copied to your ISP's computer, Internet users can see them by typing the address of the pages into their Web browsers. This address will usually be based on the ISP's own address. For example,

AOL users store their Web sites in hometown.aol.com. Similarly, CompuServe users' sites are at ourworld.compuserve.com. If you use a different ISP, check your sign-up documents for information on free

The Internet is great at giving us the opportunity to find people all over the world with similar interests. With a Web site of your own you can announce your own interests – and people will be able to find you!

Web space and addresses. If you visit one of the CompuServe sites, you'll be able to see huge categorized lists of people's Web sites and their contents (some are shown opposite). Although the space given to each site might be similar, the contents are as diverse and unique as the people who made them.

Subjects can range from *Star Trek* trivia to how to look after unusual

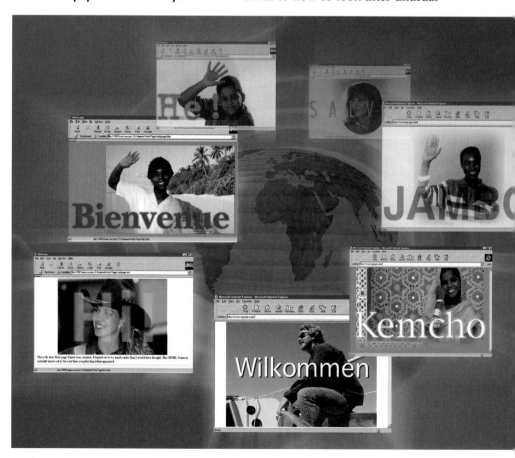

PC TIPS

To make your own Web site, you don't even need to be on the Internet! If you create a Web page and save it on your hard disk, you can simply use a Web browser to view it directly from the hard disk. You will see it exactly as it would appear if it were on the Web. This is also an excellent way of practising making a site without letting the world see your first efforts.

pets; from needlework to the fuel consumption of a 1940s roadster; or from technical PC information to Elvis' inside leg measurement.

● HTML – the Web language

The one thing that deters many people from creating a Web site is that it uses a programming language called HTML (HyperText Mark-up Language). But don't worry – HTML is one of the simplest languages in the computing world and the basics are no more complicated than typing normal text sprinkled with a few special commands.

There's no denying the fact that a page of HTML code can look complicated, but as soon as you start learning what a few of the commands mean, you'll see that everything is quite logical.

● Breaking the code

You might find yourself wondering what this odd-looking code has to do with the pictures and text you see when you type an address into your Web browser. After all, you don't see a single piece of HTML code.

What happens is that your browser strips out the HTML commands, which it uses to work out how to display the real content. The browser reads the code to work out where to place the images, words and links and displays them for the user, who need never see the underlying code that makes it possible.

The following exercises will show you how to create some simple HTML pages. When you've worked

through both of these exercises, you'll be able to put centred text on the screen, as well as pictures and even links – which are all you need to produce a perfectly usable page. In fact, many slow-loading pages are usually caused by their creator trying to use too many fancy commands.

● Begin with the basics

Learning to take full advantage of the basic HTML commands is important, not only from a technical standpoint, but also from a design one. However, once you've learnt how basic HTML works, save time and trouble by using a Web editing program, such as FrontPage Express (included with Windows 98) or Adobe PageMill. These easy-to-use programs create all the HTML code for you.

A page on the Web is a great way to let people know what's going on in a society or club, as with this page detailing the season's results in a cricket league.

You don't even have to finish the site completely before you display it to the world; a simple Under Construction graphic will let people know you're working on it.

It can be fun for a family just to introduce themselves to the world and tell other people what they are interested in. It's by no means necessary to have a complex site.

Some personal sites can have a stylish, smart appearance that differs little from the results achieved on a professional or commercial site.

Making your own Web page

It's easy to make your presence known to the world. Here, we show you how to make a start at constructing your own Web site.

1 The first thing to do with any Web page is to type the simple commands (we're using Notepad) that identify it as an HTML document. Type <HTML> on the first line and then </HTML> on the next line. The second command will let the browser know the Web page is finished. The rest of our page will be typed between these commands.

2 Now we'll create a heading for the page. Between our two lines, type another: <H1>My First Web Page!</H1>. The <H1> and </H1> commands tell the browser that the text between them is going to be the heading; it will use a bigger and bolder typeface when it displays the page.

3 Finally, type <CENTER> in front of the <H1> command and </CENTER> after </H1>. Now your text will be centred when it appears in your browser window.

4 You can now type in the main text for your Web page. Start by typing a few sentences. Begin on a new line under the heading and type as if you were typing into a word processor. However, when you get to the edge of the Notepad window press the [Enter] key to move on to a new line. Since these words come after the </H1> and </CENTER> they won't be centred or bold.

5 To finish off this simple text page, we'd like a simple line across the bottom of the page. We could add lots of underline characters, by pressing [Shift]+[-]. But there are better and more powerful options built into the HTML language. Create a new line just before the </HTML> line which finishes the page. On this new line type <HR>. This is one of the few HTML commands that doesn't need a </HR> command to switch it off.

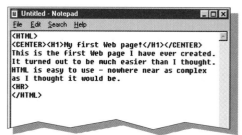

6 Now we'll save the Web page. Select Save As from the File menu, and locate a suitable folder in the Save in drop-down list. Type a simple name into the File name text box, and use an .htm extension. This file extension identifies it as an HTML file. Make sure you don't forget the full stop beforehand. Then press the Save button.

7 Now we want to see the page as it would appear on the Worldwide Web. The easiest way to load the page into your Web browser is to double-click on the My Computer icon and locate the folder on your hard disk. Find your file and double-click on it. After a few seconds your page will load into your browser and you'll see it on screen (far right). Depending on the way your browser is set up, a dialog box might appear before the page loads, asking if you want to log into your ISP – just click the Cancel button.

Adding a picture that's a link

As well as telling people all over the world about yourself, you can also show them what you look like. All you need is a picture – the rest is easy!

1 To liven up our Web page we're going to add a picture between the title and the main text. The first thing to do is find a picture. However, as Web pages use two types of picture, GIF and JPG, you might need to convert it first (see Pictures for Web sites, below). Copy the picture into the same folder you used for your Web page.

2 Now start Notepad so that you can edit the HTML file you created on the previous page. Click on the File menu and select Open. Use the Look in section of the Open dialog box to locate the relevant folder. You won't see the .htm file at first; this is because Notepad normally looks for files that end in .txt. Click on the Files of type drop-down list and select All Files (*.*). You will see your file appear, along with any others in the folder. Select the file and press the Open button.

3 Now you can edit the file. First we'll add our picture. Insert a new line under the heading and type <IMG SRC="family.jpg">, with the name of your picture in inverted commas.

4 As it is, this picture will appear at the left of the page, directly before the paragraph text. To tidy things up, place a <CENTER> command before it and </CENTER> after it. After that, create a new line and add a <BR>. This will place a space between the picture and the text.

5 We can also make the picture a clickable link. This means that when the mouse pointer of the person viewing the page moves over the picture, it will turn into a hand informing the person they can click on the picture to go to a new page. First, though, we need a second page to switch to. That's easy: we'll just edit this page and save it under a new name. Change the page to read as shown here. When you save the file in the same folder, name it link.htm.

6 Now repeat Step 2 to open the first page of your Web site again. To create the link for the picture, type <A HREF="link.htm"> before the picture command (it doesn't matter if it is before or after <CENTER>) and then type </A> after the picture. Select Save from the File menu to save these changes.

7 View your Web page by double clicking on the first Web page you created (Step 7, previous page). Your page will load with the picture in place. Click once on the picture and you'll see the second page appear. This is the principle on which the whole Web works. While there are some Web design techniques that are hard to work out, perhaps 90 per cent of all Web sites are created with commands as simple as these.

PICTURES FOR WEB SITES

Most pictures on Web sites are in GIF or JPG format. These are special formats that are suitable for use over the Internet, since they are compact and are quick to download. Other types of pictures, such as the Windows format, BMP, will need to be converted before use in your Web pages. Do this with a graphics program, such as Corel PHOTO-PAINT (see page 76).

● **About the index**
Text in italics is used for cross-references within the index (as in *see also...*). Page numbers in bold type denote the main entries for a topic.

● **Acknowledgments**

Abbreviations: t = top; b = bottom;
r = right; l = left; c = centre;
bkg = background. All cartoons
are by Chris Bramley

8	Lyndon Parker/De Agostini
9tl	Lyndon Parker/De Agostini
12	Stockmarket
13t	De Agostini
15tl	Stockmarket
16	Lyndon Parker/De Agostini
18	Lyndon Parker/De Agostini
22all	Steve Bartholomew/De Agostini
23tr	Steve Bartholomew/De Agostini
26	Steve Bartholomew/De Agostini
28	Jennie Child/De Agostini
30	Lyndon Parker/De Agostini
34	Lyndon Parker/De Agostini
38	Lyndon Parker/De Agostini
40	Lyndon Parker/De Agostini
42tall	Lyndon Parker/De Agostini
45tr	Lyndon Parker/De Agostini
46	Lyndon Parker/De Agostini
50t	Lyndon Parker/De Agostini
50b	De Agostini
53t	De Agostini
54	De Agostini
56	Lyndon Parker/De Agostini
58	Getty One Stone
60	De Agostini
62	De Agostini
64	De Agostini
66	Performing Arts Library

68	De Agostini
70	De Agostini
73	De Agostini
78	De Agostini
80	De Agostini
82	De Agostini
83all	De Agostini
85	De Agostini
86	De Agostini
87all	De Agostini
88all	De Agostini
89all	De Agostini
90	De Agostini
94	De Agostini
95all	Lyndon Parker/De Agostini
96	(elephant) Getty One Stone
96	De Agostini
97tr	(elephant) Getty One Stone
97cl,cr,bl	De Agostini
98all	Lyndon Parker/De Agostini
99all	Lyndon Parker/De Agostini
100tr	Ricoh (courtesy)
100bl	Agfa (courtesy)
101t	Lyndon Parker/De Agostini
102t	Lyndon Parker/De Agostini
102b	Ray Dunthorn/De Agostini
103all	Lyndon Parker/De Agostini
104t	(family) Imagebank
104t	(computer) Lyndon Parker/De Agostini
104c,b	Warrender Grant/De Agostini
105tl	Hewlett Parkard (courtesy)
106	Lyndon Parker/De Agostini
107all	Lyndon Parker/De Agostini
108	(dancers) Stockmarket

108	(speakers) Lyndon Parker/De Agostini
109all	Lyndon Parker/De Agostini
110t	Roland (courtesy)
110b	Lyndon Parker/De Agostini
111t	Lyndon Parker/De Agostini
111c	Yamaha (courtesy)
112	Lyndon Parker/De Agostini
113all	Lyndon Parker/De Agostini
116t	TRH Pictures
116c,bl,br	De Agostini
117tl	Aviation picture Library
117c	De Agostini
117b	TRH Pictures
118t	(picture) Bridgeman Art Library
118t	(computer) L Parker/De Agostini
118bl,br	De Agostini
119all	De Agostini
122t	D Jordan/De Agostini
123t	D Jordan/De Agostini
126all	De Agostini
130	Lyndon Parker/De Agostini
131t	Lyndon Parker/De Agostini
134	Lyndon Parker/De Agostini
138all	De Agostini
142tr,cr	Fortean Picture Library
142br	The Kobal Collection
144br	Fortean Picture Library
146	(tiger) Getty One Stone
146	(boy) Lyndon Parker/De Agostini
147t	(tiger) Getty One Stone
147t	(boy) Lyndon Parker/De Agostini
150all	Lyndon Parker/De Agostini
154all	De Agostini
157tr	Steve Bartholomew/De Agostini